A
UNIONIST
IN EAST
TENNESSEE

To Jason
Hope you enjoy the book.

Best Wishes

Marvin J. Byrd

MARVIN BYRD A ★★★★★★★★★★★★★

UNIONIST
IN EAST
TENNESSEE

★★★★★★★★★★★★★★★★★★★★★★★★★★

CAPTAIN WILLIAM K. BYRD AND THE MYSTERIOUS RAID OF 1861

Charleston  London

THE
History
PRESS

Published by The History Press
Charleston, SC 29403
www.historypress.net

First published 2011

Manufactured in the United States

ISBN 978.1.60949.245.8

Library of Congress Cataloging-in-Publication Data

Byrd, Marvin.
A Unionist in East Tennessee : Captain William K. Byrd and the mysterious raid of 1861 /
Marvin Byrd.
p. cm.
Includes bibliographical references and index.
ISBN 978-1-60949-245-8
1. Byrd, William K., ca. 1795-1861. 2. Unionists (United States Civil War)--Tennessee,
East. 3. Tennessee, East--History--Civil War, 1861-1865. 4. Secession--Tennessee. 5. Trials
I. Title.

E531.B97 2011
976.8'04--dc22

*To the Byrd families of Hawkins and Hancock Counties, Tennessee,
who stood courageously and resolutely beside our great Union during its
darkest hour.*

Contents

Acknowledgements

No matter how large or small, any effort at serious writing is seldom completed without the help and assistance of others. I wish to extend special thanks to several people whose help, influence and guidance contributed so much to this story.

To begin with, I give special recognition to grandparents William and Clara Byrd, my Tennessee connection. Although gone these many years, their memory and silent presence gave me much of the inspiration to write this story.

In addition, I give special thanks to Henry Price of Rogersville, Hawkins County, Tennessee, a retired attorney and, most recently, local county historian. A skilled and successful historical writer in his own right, Henry has written several fine works on Rogersville and Hawkins County. I had the privilege and pleasure of meeting Henry in July 1998 on my first research trip to east Tennessee. A Hawkins County native, Henry probably knows as much about the histories of Hawkins-Hancock Counties and surrounding area as anyone alive. I'm very appreciative of the many times Henry has taken to sit, talk history and answer my questions, in some instances taking precious time away from his own research and writing. Henry, whose friendship I prize, also allowed me to copy two of his maps and pointed me to several other local individuals who have played important parts in unraveling this story. Only after Henry read my first (really rough) draft of this story and offered encouragement did I begin to consider publishing it.

Another person I'm deeply indebted to is my cousin, Pat Robinson, who lives with her husband, Robert, in Harrison, Arkansas. I think she was the first person to tell me about the family tradition regarding our great-great-

Left: William Walker Byrd. Born December 14, 1860, in Lee Valley, Hawkins County, Tennessee; died January 7, 1952, in Tulsa, Oklahoma. *Courtesy of the author's collection.*

Right: Clara Moreland Howerton. Born February 11, 1876, in Mooresburg, Hawkins County, Tennessee; died August 13, 1931 in Tulsa, Oklahoma. *Courtesy of the author's collection.*

grandfather and his death at the hands of Confederate sympathizers during the Civil War, which immediately sparked my interest. Pat also located and kindly shared copies of the Civil War pension papers for James and Levi Bird, two sons of Captain William K. Byrd, which provided further information for this book and two earlier articles on the Byrd family. Last but not least, in past years Pat has provided me with little tidbits of genealogical information, graves photos, etc., that are priceless, and I'll forever be grateful.

Another person deserving special thanks is Sheila Weems Johnston, a local Hawkins County historian and writer who alerted me to the Eliza Rhea Anderson Fain diary, located at the Stamps Library in Rogersville. One evening several years ago, on a chance meeting with Sheila in the Stamps genealogy section, I casually mentioned the story about my great-great-grandfather possibly being killed or murdered by Confederate sympathizers. She then told me about seeing a reference to the "killing of old man Bird" in the Fain diary. That revelation lead to another discovery moments later when she told me about Crawford W. Hall's rare book, *Threescore Years and Ten*, located at the East Tennessee Historical Library in Knoxville, containing a second account of Byrd's death. Prior to meeting Sheila, I had been to the Stamps library numerous times doing research, reviewing microfilm, and I had seen the Fain diary but for some reason had failed to review the rich information contained within its pages; thanks to Sheila, that quickly changed.

Also deserving special credit is Haynes and Opal Alvis, who my wife and I consider some of the nicest people anywhere. Haynes and Opal, both retired, have served faithfully on the Hawkins County Genealogical and Historical Society board for many years. They've written numerous articles on Hawkins County history and continue to publish the society's widely known and highly respected quarterly, *Distant Crossroads*, which is only one of their many projects over the years. Without a doubt, Haynes and Opal have contributed greatly to the written and published history of Hawkins County. It was Haynes who discovered the "indictment for the murder of William K. Byrd" in some old Hawkins County court papers and passed it along, adding significantly to this work. On other occasions—countless to remember—they have offered important suggestions and ideas for my research, for which I'm immensely grateful. Lastly, I thank them for being so kind to my wife and me, inviting us on several occasions into their home and for showing us the best eating places around Hawkins County.

Still, there are others deserving credit, such as cousin Arlie Drinnon, who lives with his son in Pumpkin Valley along Byrd Creek in northern Hawkins County. Thanks to Arlie, I learned of the existence and directions to the "second Byrd cemetery." This cemetery is a possible resting place for Captain William K. Byrd. Besides cousin Arlie, others deserving special mention are Elaine and Ron Highsmith, owners of the property where the second Byrd cemetery and former home of William E. Byrd is situated. Ron and Elaine have been so kind and cooperative for a number of years, allowing myself and others onto their property periodically to clean, mow, catalog graves and do restoration on the cemetery, even replacing the cemetery fence and gate several years ago.

Then there is Danette Welch, a reference assistant with the Calvin M. McClung Historical Collection in Knoxville, who, shortly after a conversation regarding my research, just happened to notice an old *Knoxville Whig* newspaper article about Joseph B. Heiskell that mentioned "the bird raid." Danette notified me via e-mail of her discovery, for which I'm very grateful. Along with Danette, there is also Sally Polhemus, also a staff person with the McClung Historical Collection, who located and provided me with a very rare photo of Joseph Brown Heiskell.

Most of all, I want to thank my dear wife, Mary, the love of my life, who has allowed me to be away from home for many hours—even weeks at a time—doing research for this story and other projects. Mary has always encouraged and supported my efforts to unravel and finish the story of William K. Byrd, for which I'm sincerely thankful. Without her loving support, I could never have completed the untold story of Captain William K. Byrd, an east Tennessee Unionist.

Sincere thanks and gratitude to all,
Marvin Byrd

Introduction

According to census records, William K. Byrd[1] (1795-1802–died December 7, 1861) was born in North Carolina[2] and later moved with his family at a young age to the Hawkins County, Tennessee area. His father is believed to be James Bird, who is on the tax list of Captain Looney's company for Hawkins County in 1810.[3] Captain Looney is believed to be Absolum Looney, the sheriff of Hawkins County from 1807 to 1812.

Around 1816, William K. married Pheba "Phoebe" Reynolds[4] (1800-1803–died?). No marriage record for William K. and Pheba is known to exist in Hawkins County records or elsewhere, for that matter. Although some evidence (see note 2) suggests William and Phoebe were originally from Barren County, Kentucky, where marriage and census records indicate several Byrd (Burd) and Reynolds families lived in close proximity and intermarried from about 1797 to after 1810.

William and Phoebe had the following children: James Anderson Bird (September 29, 1818–December 2, 1871), William Elliott "Ellie" Byrd (about 1823-1824–January 18, 1898), Malinda Byrd (about 1825–died?), Ephraim Byrd (about 1830–about 1865), Andrew Jackson Byrd (about 1832 or 1833–after 1880) and Levi Benjamin Bird (February 15, 1836–November 1, 1924).[5] Along with the above offspring, there appears to have been two other female children noted in the 1830 and 1840 censuses, born about 1817 and 1827. Unfortunately, their identities are unknown at this time.

Also obscure are William's personal life and beliefs before the Civil War. Other than census records and a few land deeds, no personal documents, letters or commentaries have apparently survived to the present day.

What follows, regarding William's Civil War involvement and death in early December 1861, are for the most part from various public records or third-party accounts. Foremost are the grand jury indictment and other legal records from the Hawkins County Circuit Court, assorted newspaper articles, the Hancock County Chancery Court records, three third-party accounts and the pension papers of his eldest son, James Anderson Bird.

William's life, like so many others living in America during the chaotic times of 1860–1870, was overshadowed and significantly impacted by the greater historical events of that period. The story of Captain William K. Byrd personified this reality. Therefore, any personal narrative from this period demands first an overview of those greater historical events, particularly those occurring in east Tennessee from June to December 1861. By understanding and appreciating these wider events, we can achieve a deeper or more insightful look into William K. Byrd's own life and those around him. Only then can we hope to understand the life and times of Captain William K. Byrd, an east Tennessee Unionist.

CHAPTER 1

Prelude to Terror

On May 27, 1861, with the all-important Tennessee secession referendum vote only days away, the east Tennessee town of Elizabethton, Carter County, became the scene of a rousing public debate, as reported by the secessionist newspaper, the *Knoxville Register*. On the "Separation side," Joseph Brown Heiskell, a Hawkins County resident, and William M. Cocke of Grainger County opposed William Blount Carter and Nathaniel G. Taylor of Carter County, who favored remaining in the Union. Speaking first, Joseph Heiskell, or Major Heiskell, as most acquaintances commonly addressed him, stated that "he had been a union man until all hope was lost by the usurpation of unconstitutional power by the administration in Washington." Heiskell went on to denounce Abraham Lincoln, stating his use of power to call out the militias was not what our forefathers intended and "clearly showed what an enormous stretch of power he [Lincoln] had assumed unto himself." Offering other comments on taxes and the "use of coercion," Heiskell stated "that the government in the hands of the bastard, rump President was despotism, an engine of oppression."

William B. Carter followed Heiskell to the podium and, according to the news article, treated Major Heiskell with personal respect but displayed bitterness in denunciating Jeff Davis and the Confederate States. Carter claimed he had voted for John Fremont in 1856 and personally denied accusations of being a "black republican." But responding to these claims, the article reported Carter had forgotten telling "the people some time ago that he preferred Lincoln to John Bell" in the 1860 election.[6]

Of course the debate that day in Elizabethton solved little or changed many hearts and minds regarding the secession crisis. Heiskell and Cocke, seemingly on a public speaking tour for several weeks in support of secession, had presented similar speeches in Grainger County earlier that month. But at this late date in 1861, with the pending state referendum on secession only days away, common ground clearly lacked between opposing sides. In fact, after the fall of Fort Sumter, many people had become polarized in their viewpoints and stands on critical political issues. Of course, at the time, no better examples of this polarization could be found than Joseph B. Heiskell and William B. Carter. Believing strongly in their respective viewpoints, they were destined to play pivotal roles in the coming conflict in east Tennessee. Few knew or even suspected at the time, but Carter, as a leading Unionist organizer, and Heiskell, as secessionist leader and later Confederate congressman, would ultimately exert enormous and far-reaching impact on the lives of east Tennesseans before the war was very old.

On Saturday, June 8, 1861, Tennessee voted to secede from the Union, the eleventh and final state to officially leave, but voters in the eastern third of the state rejected the idea by a vote of two to one. Soon after the state referendum on secession, Thomas A.R. Nelson, a U.S. congressman from Tennessee, led a convention of 285 Union, or Loyalist, delegates on June 17 in the town of Greeneville, about sixty miles east of Knoxville. Nelson's intent was to convince supporters to take a hard line with Confederate authorities. Among his proposals, he urged delegates not to abide by the new "Declaration of Independence" adopted by the secessionist-controlled Tennessee legislature. He also pleaded with representatives for their

Thomas A.R. Nelson, while personally shocked by Lincoln's call for troops, remained strongly against secession leading up to the war. *Courtesy of Library of Congress.*

respective counties "to legally and constitutionally continue in the Union as the State of Tennessee" and resist by force any effort by Confederates to station rebel troops in their midst.[7]

After heated debate and some delegates fearing reprisal by Confederate authorities, the body ultimately rejected Nelson's proposals, deeming them too extreme. Instead, the convention concluded by adopting a less inflammatory "Declaration of Grievances," which included a resolution to petition the state legislature seeking permission for east Tennessee to form a new state. Soon after on June 29, the legislature rejected the separate statehood petition authored at the Greeneville convention, saying it failed to represent "the true sentiments of the masses of East Tennessee."[8]

So with the secessionist-controlled Tennessee legislature having rebuffed these latest efforts, many Union sympathizers now felt their lives threatened and endangered, causing many families to soon pack up and leave the state to avoid taking up arms against their political beliefs. Others, mainly fathers and sons, opted to leave families behind and go silently into the night to join Union army regiments that were then forming in Kentucky. During the next four years, some thirty thousand Union supporters, traveling mostly on foot, would ultimately cross over the Cumberland Mountains to join loyal Tennessee regiments in southeastern Kentucky and fight against the Confederacy. Still, other Loyalists decided to stay put and defend home and hearth against what they perceived as the growing Rebel threat. This latter group soon started organizing militias, or home guards, training forces of up to five hundred men and openly threatening armed resistance to the Confederacy.

Even before the Unionist Greeneville convention in June, Confederate authorities had come to view the growing Union partisan activity, now well underway in east Tennessee, as a growing major concern. Birthed during those early days of the secession crisis, this partisan—or in some cases, outright guerrilla—activity during the summer of 1861 would ultimately intensify, taking on its own life and personality and, in effect, creating a "second front" in the war between the North and South. During the coming conflict, great military armies lead by men like Robert E. Lee, U.S. Grant and others would battle face to face and toe to toe, but in the midst of it all, another war would be waged closer to home in the backwoods, valleys and mountains of east Tennessee and other isolated areas of southern Appalachia.

The "second front" between the North and South was destined to evolve into a "war in the night," in many ways fought by an unseen enemy—a "war at every door," as one author described it, a war more

This woodcut from *Harper's Weekly* depicts east Tennessee Union men meeting secretly and swearing allegiance. *Courtesy of Library of Congress.*

basic, raw and brutal in nature. In fact, this partisan fighting between Rebels and Loyalists on the homefront would outlive the war and continue seemingly unabated for a significant period after the war's official conclusion. Once Tennessee seceded from the Union, escalating violence between Union and Confederate partisans quickly festered into an open sore, sticking in the side of Confederacy for the war's duration, never fully being rectified.

One of the leading Confederates of east Tennessee, Landon Carter Haynes of Carter County, predicted very early on a Unionist uprising when he wrote on July 6, 1861, to then Confederate secretary of war Leroy P. Walker:

> *Mr. Brownlow in his paper* [William G. "Parson" Brownlow, a leading Tennessee Unionist and editor of the *Knoxville Whig*], *says civil war is inevitable…and that Union men have 10,000 men under drill and armed with rifles and shotguns.*

Haynes went on to say that "the New York Times, in a lengthily article, say East Tennessee is a vital point in the Lincoln Government; and urges Union men to seize Knoxville, and hold it till Lincoln can give aid."[9]

Landon Carter Haynes's dire warning to Southern authorities of a possible attack on the bridges of east Tennessee fell on deaf ears. Haynes later became a Confederate senator. *Courtesy of Tennessee State Library and Archives.*

Besides Haynes, other prominent secessionists, such as William Swan, John Crozier Ramsey, William McAdoo and J.G.M. Ramsey, along with Confederate military figures, urged Confederate president Jefferson Davis to take immediate action against Unionists. But despite these growing concerns by leading secessionists and increasing violence on the part of Unionists during the early summer of 1861, Confederate authorities made little or no effort to impose their will over east Tennessee Loyalists immediately after the June secession vote. Many secessionists still held the belief that Unionists could eventually be persuaded by leniency to embrace the Southern cause.

On August 1, 1861, east Tennesseans went to the polls to vote on three things: to cast ballots either for or against a new Confederate constitution, elect a governor and choose candidates for the new Confederate Congress. But results of the election infuriated and angered most secessionist leaders, including Tennessee governor Isham Harris. In effect, the election was used by east Tennesseans to demonstrate opposition to Confederate rule by rejecting the Confederate constitution by 68 percent and similarly opposing the election of Harris for governor. But strong returns from west and middle Tennessee secured reelection for Harris despite the opposition and disappointing numbers from east Tennessee. Beyond this lack of support for Harris, east Tennessee voters showed further distain for secessionism by openly electing three Unionist congressional candidates in the three easternmost districts of Tennessee. Unionist Thomas A.R. Nelson, a leader at the Greeneville convention, was

President Jefferson Davis. East
Tennessee Unionists may not have
been his biggest headache but possibly
the most frustrating. It created
problems for the Confederacy during
the entire war. *Courtesy of Tennessee State
Library and Archives.*

elected to the First District seat, while George Bridges went to the Third
District seat and Andrew J. Clements to the Fourth District. After the
election, all three immediately added insult to injury, attempting to escape
from the Confederacy to represent their districts in Washington, D.C., which
further angered Confederate authorities.[10] Clements actually made it to
Washington and was seated by the U.S. Congress, while Bridges and Nelson
were captured by Confederates.

But after the August elections, Unionists continued to openly defy and
resist Confederate rule, with many east Tennessee political leaders refusing
to fully embrace the Confederacy. Infuriated and angered, Southern leaders
now became convinced they had to alter their policies. So on August 16,
1861, Governor Harris announced a new and stronger policy of repressing
"loyalists" by arresting hundreds of Unionists. Almost immediately, in
response to the arrests, William G. Brownlow began calling for revenge
in his editorials from his Knoxville newspaper, the last Unionist journal in
the South. He also boldly encouraged Union men to "hold themselves in
readiness for action, action, action."[11]

As the unfolding events of August continued to heat up, the Confederate
War Department quickly ordered several regiments of Confederate
soldiers into the area in support of the stronger policy by Harris and other
secessionists. Soon, the eastern counties of Tennessee had over ten thousand
soldiers guarding key railroad bridges, supply depots and other important

Governor Isham G. Harris, an ardent Southern supporter, used his lofty political position to promote and push Tennessee toward eventual secession. *Courtesy of Tennessee State Library and Archives.*

sites.[12] General Felix Zollicoffer, the Confederate military leader responsible for implementing the new, more aggressive policies, had only taken charge of the east Tennessee district on August 1, the day of the elections. Zollicoffer had been a journalist, state senator and U.S. congressman before the war.

New Confederate secretary of war Judah P. Benjamin, having taken over only recently from Leroy P. Walker, initially ordered Zollicoffer to secure the rail lines

William G. "Parson" Brownlow, while resisting Rebels, would be threatened, beaten, shot, sued, hanged in effigy, indicted, imprisoned and exiled but never silenced. *Courtesy of Tennessee State Library and Archives.*

and prevent the North from smuggling arms into the region, to break up Loyalist political and military organizations and, if necessary, aid civilian authorities in suppressing Loyalist treason activities. At the same time, Benjamin asked Zollicoffer to do whatever he could to win over rebellious Loyalists. But given these conflicting goals, it appears Benjamin left it up to Zollicoffer to determine exactly how his directives were to be implemented.

Within days of taking command, Zollicoffer issued a proclamation to the people of east Tennessee in which he set forth his policy to civilians. First he stated he would not tolerate any treasonous activities by citizens, and that the Confederate government considered the June referendum final and binding on all citizens, regardless of their political beliefs. He also indicated Loyalists would be left basically in a state of neutrality, explaining that "no man's rights, property, or privileges shall be disturbed. All who desire peace can have peace, by quietly and harmlessly pursuing their lawful avocation."

In effect, Zollicoffer stated a willingness to tolerate Unionists as long as they didn't commit treason. No doubt aware of the unique challenges facing him in east Tennessee, this initial, rather conciliatory approach, by General Zollicoffer toward Loyalists would ultimately put him at odds with the stronger secessionist element in east Tennessee.[13] This lenient approach, appreciated by some Loyalists, was destined to be blamed by the Swan, McAdoo and Ramsey crowd as contributing to the full-scale Unionist uprising later that fall.

Brigadier General Felix K. Zollicoffer was placed on the hot seat in August 1861, becoming senior Confederate officer in east Tennessee. As a result, he received far more blame for not controlling Loyalists than deserved. *Courtesy of Tennessee State Library and Archives.*

But by late summer of 1861, east Tennessee Unionists had no intention of turning back, despite any leniency shown by Confederate authorities. With escalating activities bordering on treason growing daily, Unionists seemed more intent on renouncing and resisting the Confederacy by any means possible. In reality, the second front of the Civil War was on the verge of becoming a firestorm. Plus, as Unionists began to experience the full impact of increased presence of Southern troops in east Tennessee and the stronger policies enacted by authorities, any hope now for a peaceful solution seemed all but impossible.

To make matters worst, a wave of confidence quickly spread among secessionists and Confederate supporters, encouraging them to extreme arrogance in their treatment of Union men. The Confederate victory at the first Bull Run on July 21, 1861, fueled much of this maltreatment. This Confederate victory in effect, along with the stronger policies after August 1, served to stir up old hatreds and ill feelings by Confederates against Union people.[14] This abuse became more prevalent and particularly harsh in the country areas of east Tennessee. In fact, it seemed the most honorable of Confederate men didn't consider it degrading to inform on their Union neighbors. Time and again, normal friendships and personal kinship were being disregarded. Men otherwise mild mannered now frequently became anxious for the blood of Unionist men.[15]

In late August, the Provisional Confederate Congress passed the Alien Enemies Act, adding further to the lockdown on Loyalist activities. This act basically ordered any citizen hostile to the Confederacy to remove themselves within forty days or thereafter be subject to apprehension and forced removal as alien enemies. In addition to this measure, another act soon followed; a Sequestration Act that permitted the confiscation of all real property owned by "alien enemies." For east Tennessee Union people, both acts created serious problems and added greatly to escalating tensions between the two sides.

During August, local "Lincolnites," (a term used by Confederates to refer to and disparage Loyalists) in Carter County began making "large and bloody threats" against local secessionists, such as to "tear up the railroad from Knoxville to Bristol, burn the property of southern men, and take all... leading secessionist(s) prisoner." It was about this same time that noted Carter County Unionist Nathaniel G. Taylor, under accusation by Confederates for involvement in the plots, sought refuge in the mountains.[16] Confederates later arrested Taylor and attempted to try him as an accomplice in the bridge burnings, but the trial ended in acquittal. In Union County, another hotbed for Loyalist activity, local secessionists claimed they were being ruled by local Lincoln supporters and sympathizers with a "rod of iron." Possibly to defuse this tense situation, Confederates arrested Union County Unionist leader Dr. John W. Thornburgh and several other men. Soon after, authorities took Thornburgh and the others to Knoxville for court appearances before the East Tennessee Confederate District Court in September. Thornburgh was eventually imprisoned in Nashville.[17]

In late April, 1861, over in Hawkins County shortly after the fall of Fort Sumter, a meeting billed as involving "a large and respectable portion of the citizens of the vicinity" met to consider its response and prompt action "to the alarming state of the country." The attendants selected James Amis as chairman and Littleton H. Rogan, a thirty-seven-year-old local merchant, as secretary. Both men lived in close proximity in the Lyon's Store area of District Seven of Hawkins County, along with two other members of the group, Eldridge Hord, age fifty-nine, and Robert Cooper, age fifty-two, both wealthy farmers. In fact, James Amis, age twenty-one, a saddler, according to 1860 census records, lived with the Eldridge Hord family. The remaining members of the group hailed from the New Canton area of Hawkins County; they included David Lyons, Colonel Nat Wells and John S. Hamilton, age thirty-one, a farmer.

It's not known exactly how many Hawkins County residents actually participated in the meeting nor the personal political makeup of those attending, but the resulting resolutions voted on and put forth that day at New Canton were clearly prosecessionist. Among the resolutions agreed upon was that Tennessee should "take immediate steps to dissolve all connections with the Lincoln government" and neither give "tribute or money or men" to "the Black Republicans," and they "welcomed the Black Republican invaders of southern soil" in their "effort to subjugate the south with Bloody hands to Hospitable Graves."

Colonel Carrick White Heiskell, brother of Joseph B. Heiskell, served with Company K, Nineteenth Tennessee Infantry, CSA., enlisted as private and rose to colonel. After the war, he moved to Memphis like his brother. *Courtesy of Worsham, Old Nineteenth.*

Their final resolution put forth proposed the organization of a military company to uphold the various resolutions.[18]

By early May 1861, following the New Canton resolutions, Southern supporters in Hawkins County organized the first local Confederate company, called the Hawkins Boys. Confederate authorities would later muster this unit into the Confederate army as Company K, Nineteenth Tennessee Infantry, CSA. The Hawkins Boys arrived in Knoxville by train on May 15, 1861, with seventy-two men and commanding officers Captain Abraham Fulkerson and First Lieutenant Carrick Heiskell, brother of Joseph Brown Heiskell. Along with this unit, a Knoxville newspaper at the time reported two other Confederate military units already in the formulation stages in Hawkins County.[19] The article failed to mention the name of those units.

In the Hancock County area of upper East Tennessee in June 1861, a man named G. Fain (George Fain) provided evidence of rising Union partisan activity around the Hancock area in a letter to his brother, Commissary General Richard Fain of the Provisional Army of Tennessee. The letter outlined the need of "forming a volunteer [Confederate] company on the north side of Clinch Mountain, by the name of the Clinch Mountain Rangers."

Clinch Mountain represents the geographical boundary line separating the two counties and cuts northeast to southwest across northern Hawkins County. The town of Sneedville in Hancock County lies a few miles north of Clinch Mountain along the Clinch River, while the town of Rogersville, located in Hawkins County, lies south of Clinch and about thirty miles southeast of Sneedville. Fain went on to tell his brother Richard, "It is of the utmost importance that we should have our arms as quick as possible.

Richard Fain, husband of Eliza Fain, was a graduate of U.S. Military Academy in 1832 and served as an officer in the Confederate commissary. *From* Sanctified Trial, The Diary of Eliza Rhea Anderson Fain, a Confederate Woman in East Tennessee, *with permission of the University of Tennessee Press, Knoxville.*

The union men on the north side of C. Mo [Clinch Mountain] are arming themselves for rebellion."[20]

A month later, on July 24, in another letter to General Richard Fain, a Lewis S. Poats of Hawkins County offered the services of the Clinch Mountain Rangers to the state, apparently the same Confederate company mentioned in George Fain's letter. Ultimately, this same Rangers company with Captain H.C. Gillespie commanding, consisting of recruits from Hawkins, Hancock and Lee Counties, Virginia, would march into Knoxville the third week of August 1861. The Clinch Mountain Rangers are later mustered into the Confederate army as Company D, Fifth (McClellan's) Tennessee Cavalry Battalion, CSA[21] and commanded by Henry K. Legg. On arrival in Knoxville that late August day, an article in the secessionist *Knoxville Register* noted that the Rangers "had stood up manfully for their principles…as evidence of their devotion to the southern cause…We trust the boys of Clinch River will fill up their ranks of this company, and enroll themselves among the patriots, now risking their lives in defense of Southern homes and hearthstones."[22]

Also during this period, General Richard Fain with his wife, Eliza Rhea Anderson Fain, and family lived only a short distance from Rogersville in Hawkins County. Eliza, a very religious Southern lady and consistent supporter of secession, along with her husband and family, kept a detailed diary during the war and for most of her married life. Eliza and Richard had six sons, five of which served in the Confederate army along with Richard.

Eliza noted in her personal diary on Tuesday, July 23, 1861, "A difficulty was likely to occur in Sneedville [Hancock County] that the Union men were or had taken H. Rose's company of volunteers' prisoners."

If the "H. Rose" identification is correct, it may be a reference to Sergeant Henry C. Rose, who served with Company K, Nineteenth Tennessee Infantry, CSA, aka the Hawkins Boys, enlisting in May 1861, or Private

Eliza Rhea Anderson Fain, a pious, church-going, religious and educated lady, was the mother of thirteen children. She, like her husband, strongly supported the Southern cause and its ideals. *From* Sanctified Trial, The Diary of Eliza Rhea Anderson Fain, a Confederate Woman in East Tennessee, *with permission of the University of Tennessee Press, Knoxville.*

Henry C. Rose, a member of Company I, Twenty-ninth Tennessee Infantry, CSA.[23] Also with this altercation taking place in Sneedville, it's suspected Henry did in fact, as noted in census, belong to the family of William S. Rose, a known secessionist and fairly well-to-do local merchant who lived in Sneedville. William's youthful son, Henry, would have been about age seventeen or eighteen at the time. Eliza, writing again the following day, Wednesday, July 24, 1861, noted that "the rumors of war make us feel uneasy. The difficulty is still existing in Sneedville."[24]

Apparently Confederate authorities eventually defused the tense situation Eliza spoke of in her diary; it amounted to an apparent standoff in Hancock County between rival Unionist and secessionist home guard units, with each side numbering several hundred, gathered in nearby camps.[25]

Possibly shedding further light on the above episode is information provided by Alton L. Greene, a historian and genealogist, in an article titled "Hancock County Tennessee: The County That Time Forgot," published a few years ago.[26] In the article, Greene recounts a Civil War clash between Unionists and a group of Southern supporters who attempted to meet in Sneedville soon after Tennessee's secession for the purpose of forming a

Confederate company. According to Greene, the company in question would become the basis for Company D, Twenty-ninth Tennessee Infantry, CSA.

While the event described by Greene may not in fact be the same event Eliza Fain noted in her diary, the striking similarities and timing of the two stories make it highly probable. According to Greene, the captain of this group or future Confederate company is simply identified as "Captain Rose," with the group's members made up of about twenty young Hancock County men. Greene noted that this precarious affair started one evening after a prospective company recruit—a member of the local secessionist Cantwell family—had "words with a man named Barton" earlier in the day while on his way to the Rebel meeting. The man, whom Greene called Barton, is believed to be Charles L. Barton, a local Hancock Unionist leader and representative to the Greeneville convention the previous June. Barton is described by Greene as a "Northern man by birth and education, and a known Abolitionist." According to Greene, the argument between the two men ended with Cantwell administering a good "whipping" of Barton, causing Barton to hurriedly leave Sneedville while "swearing vengeance on all Rebels and Rebel sympathizers."

But around midnight came word to Captain Rose that Unionists had surrounded Sneedville, and they were asking Rose and his men to surrender unconditionally or face certain death. Soon after, Rose and his men took refuge in the Sneedville courthouse, a brick structure, and quickly prepared for their defense. Greene further indicated that the 20 men and their families "were about all the Confederates that were in the county" at the time. Greene goes on to relate that "Barton had at least 500 men," with additional Unionist "reinforcements being received by the firing of guns and the lighting of signals." According to Greene, the "true color" of Hancock men were now being shown, and "they were overwhelmingly Union colors." But within hours, several of the Confederates slipped away from the courthouse to warn friends and family of the pending crisis.

The next day, units of the Confederate military responded with a show of force by assembling one thousand men at Mulberry Gap under the command of a Lieutenant Bishop, believed to be William P. Bishop, later captain of Company D, Twenty-ninth Infantry Regiment, CSA. Along with this company, a second Confederate unit located on the Virginia-Tennessee border under the command of a General C. Johnson was placed on alert, with the unit being only a short distance from the pending crisis in Sneedville. A third unit—a Confederate cavalry detachment under the command of a Colonel Walker—managed to arrive on the scene from Cumberland Gap the very same night, which no doubt did more than anything to defuse the volatile situation. According to Greene, once Barton became aware of the reinforcements and actions by Confederates, he quietly withdrew his men, thereby ending the whole affair.

In summary and as noted, it's felt that the events depicted by Eliza and Mr. Greene are in fact the same event, taking place on July 23–24, 1861. Also, Captain Rose in Greene's story may very well have not been "H. Rose or Henry C. Rose," as implied in Eliza's retelling, but rather its more likely "Captain Rose" in both Greene and Eliza's stories referred to Henry's older brother, James G. Rose, who did in fact serve as a captain, according to Tennessee civil war records, of D Company, Twenty-ninth Infantry. As far as the actual number of Confederates and Unionists involved in the July fracas in Sneedville, this is hard to gauge. One commentary suggested several hundred gathered in rival camps, but, of course, this is much higher than Greene's account of there being barely twenty Confederates, including their families in the whole county.[27]

Further aggravating tensions in Hancock County during July and August 1861 were rampant rumors among secessionists accusing local Loyalist leaders Joel W. Jarvis, captain of a local unionist company, and C.L. Barton, the local Unionist representative to the Greeneville convention, of secretly organizing and plotting with others in open defiance of Confederates. Of course, the man Barton is believed the same as noted in the Alton Greene story. Southern supporters claimed Jarvis and Barton had traveled to Kentucky to "consult with the minions of Lincoln and his man Friday, Andy Johnson" and had returned to solicit others to join their "treasonous expedition."[28]

As fear and panic spread in Hancock and northern Hawkins Counties, Southern sympathizers in Sneedville in August petitioned Confederate commander Brigadier General Felix Zollicoffer to station troops in their town. In a letter addressed from F.M. Turner, a local Sneedville wagon maker, to Zollicoffer, Turner wrote, "We are threatened with immediate invasion from the Union party of Hancock and Hawkins, and perhaps other counties in East Tennessee in connection with Union and Northern men from some of the mountainous counties of Kentucky." Consequently, Turner noted, "We do not feel that the lives of ourselves and our families are by any means safe."

Building further his case for military intervention, Turner offered stronger statements by the local Hancock sheriff as proof of this "eminent threat." He told Zollicoffer about a "strong force from Kentucky," escorted by Union men from Hancock County and supported by five hundred local Unionists from Hancock and Hawkins Counties, that planned to soon advance on the area with intentions of destroying the railroad and halting transportation on the east Tennessee and Virginia line.[29] These alarming details and possible plot divulged by the Hancock sheriff looked strikingly similar to another Unionist plan. In fact, it was similar to the one noted Loyalist William Blount Carter would carry out barely three months later on November 8, 1861.

Complicating even further these growing tensions in Hancock County and all across east Tennessee during the summer of 1861 were rumors of Confederates being shot at and even killed by "Tories" and Loyalist "tampering with slaves." Thus as the fears of local citizens continued escalating daily from the violent acts and disturbing activity, local secessionists soon lost patience with Zollicoffer, ultimately "going over his head" and beseeching Richmond directly for martial law.[30] These random and covert acts of violence would graphically characterize this expanding "second front" of the Civil War, not just in east Tennessee but much of the southern Appalachians. The local Hancock County situation only mirrored the ever growing tensions between Confederates and Unionists all over east Tennessee

By late August, and responding apparently to the repeated pleas for help and stronger policies, Rebel authorities in Hancock and Hawkins Counties arrested several suspected Loyalists thought to be involved in the treasonous activities. As many as 15 to 16 men from Hancock and Hawkins Counties, along with several from Greene and Union Counties, were taken into custody and marched off to Knoxville. Upon arrival in Knoxville, these captives, with other east Tennesseans, were imprisoned to await trial before the East Tennessee Confederate District Court, opening in September 1861. During the fall term of this court, 109 civilians from east Tennessee, including those from Hancock and Hawkins Counties, were ultimately charged with various "alleged acts of disloyalty." The mass arrests of Unionists, while seemingly significant at the time in the ongoing Confederate crackdown, would soon pale in comparison to the calamity and deadly terror Confederates would unleash against them later that fall.

CHAPTER 2

"Indiscriminate Arrests"

B y September 1861, Knoxville, Tennessee, was a town clearly divided politically and would remain so for most of the Civil War. While most observers considered Nashville and Memphis in west Tennessee "hotbeds" for secession, Knoxville remained a town split between the two fractions. The secession vote back in June demonstrated this division, with local Knoxville voters narrowly passing the referendum. Also by this time, Knoxville secessionists should have been in a better mood, with the stronger Confederate policies instituted against revolting Unionists after the August elections; but that wasn't necessarily so. Some local secessionists like William McAdoo repeatedly complained about the "lenient policies" of Confederate general Felix Zollicoffer, stating Zollicoffer "is proving himself totally unfit for the duty of quelling this Lincolnism in East Tennessee."

In early August, shortly after Zollicoffer assumed command in Knoxville, McAdoo had commented that Zollicoffer was spending way too much time patrolling the Tennessee border and not enough time rounding up local Unionists.

On the other side, leading Knoxville Unionists since August had tried to discourage Confederates from their heavy-handed policies against Loyalists by voicing concern and strong disagreement regarding the harsh treatment. Local Unionists also tried to play down and even ridicule treasonous activities by Loyalists as even happening to the extent claimed by Confederate authorities. In fact, soon after the August elections, William G. Brownlow, the fire-breathing local Unionist newspaperman, adopted a milder or more conciliatory tone in his attacks on secessionists from his *Knoxville Whig* editorial pages. This conciliatory tone by Brownlow and other local Unionists may have resulted from several things, including the growing presence of Confederate troops in Knoxville and the surrounding area resulting from the crackdown; from realization that stronger policies recently instituted by Confederates made it fruitless to fight any longer; and possibly from the sheer fear of being arrested and tried for possible treason before the East Tennessee Confederate District Court, which would open soon in Knoxville. Also by September 1861, so-called political prisoners already under arrest from outlying areas of east Tennessee for alleged crimes of disloyalty were routinely being marched through the streets almost daily, filling the Knoxville jail for several weeks leading up to the opening of the court. The stark reality of what life had now become no doubt had a sobering impact on the hearts and minds of local Unionists like Brownlow, possibly tempering their zeal for Unionism and causing them for the sake of their own self-survival to rein in their public expressions of contempt and hatred for the Confederacy. In reality, all of the above probably played a role in quelling the mood of local Knoxville Unionists during this period.[31]

On Thursday, September 6, the Confederate District Court for East Tennessee opened in Knoxville with Judge West H. Humphreys presiding over the first session of the court since Tennessee's secession. The court would hold its inaugural session in temporary quarters located in the Knox County Courthouse. Before the war, Judge Humphreys, a native Tennessean, served as Tennessee attorney general and reporter of cases for the state Supreme Court from 1839 to 1851. Later, in 1853, President Franklin Pierce appointed him a federal judge for Tennessee, where he served until the war opened. Shortly after, Humphreys, a secessionist supporter, received an appointment from President Jefferson Davis as judge of the East Tennessee Confederate District Court.[32] But despite his apparent support for secession, Humphreys, during this September term of the court, would prove far more lenient and benevolent toward Loyalist defendants than many would have liked, especially his district attorney, John Crozier Ramsey. Ramsey was a strong secessionist who harbored intense feelings against Unionists and lacked sympathy for their so-called "treasonable activities."

In addition to Judge Humphreys, other officials of the court included General J.B. Clements, Confederate marshal for east Tennessee; William C. Kain, clerk, age thirty-six; and, of course, John Crozier Ramsey as district attorney—another Davis appointee.

According to court minutes, Crozier, with seventeen other attorneys, is noted as being authorized to practice in this initial session of the court. The other attorneys included Robert B. Reynolds; Joseph Brown Heiskell,; M. Jarnagin (Jarnigan?); W.M. Churchwell; T.J. Campbell; S.L. Finley; a man by the last name of Mynatt, believed to be John H. Mynatt; H.S. Mehaffey; C.M. Alexander; John Baxter; J.F.J. Servis; Henry Elliot; George W. Churchwell; A.A. Doak; John H. Crozier; William G. Swan; and William G. McAdoo. This group acted as a pool of defense attorneys, which the court apparently offered or assigned in some cases to represent defendants.[33]

Later in January 1862, these original attorneys were supplemented by others sworn to practice in the court. They included Oliver P. Temple; M. Thornburg, believed to be Montgomery Thornburg; James R. Cocke; Samuel A. Rogers; W.C. Kyle; John B. Hoyle (Hoyl?); John H. Sawyers; R.M. Edwards; and Samuel A. Smith.[34] Of this latter group, Temple may have been the most notable—a Unionist who held moderate views and was considered by most as a key east Tennessee Unionist leader with the likes of Horace Maynard, Andrew Johnson and William G. Brownlow. Others such as Thornburg, Hoyle and Smith were all considered Unionists or possessed sympathetic views. Thornburg, a Union leader and speaker from Jefferson County, later succumbed to arrest and imprisonment for his Unionist support, ultimately dying in prison. Another man in this group, W.C. Kyle, a former Union representative for Hawkins and Hancock Counties at the Knoxville and Greeneville conventions, had sons who either served in the Confederate army or government.[35]

A more important factor or daunting reality for Unionists awaiting trial that September related to the initial group of attorneys authorized in September 1861. This group included several hard-core secessionists who not only lacked sympathy for Unionist viewpoints, but in some cases they had expressed outright animosity for Tories. In fact, several of these men were some of the strongest supporters of the Southern cause found anywhere in the state at that time. For example, District Attorney John Crozier Ramsey, considered by some as an "original secessionist," along with William G. Swan, a former state attorney general, and John H. Crozier, an ex-member of Congress, all had previously spoken out in favor of stronger or harsher policies against Unionists. Also, John H. Cozier, a politically influential man, held membership in a small group of young professionals in Knoxville who favored dissolution of the Union. Among Crozier, Swan and Ramsey, the three strongly supported dissolution from the start of the "secession crisis" soon after Lincoln's election. But now

Ramsey, emboldened and in a position of authority as district attorney, sought to apply the harshest measures possible against Tories, many arrested based on affidavits written by Ramsey himself.

Still others of the group like William G. McAdoo, Joseph B. Heiskell and William M. Churchwell were all committed secessionists and strong advocates for severe measures against loyalists. In particular, Heiskell was destined to gain a level of infamous notoriety for his wartime service, at least among Unionists. In Oliver Temple's book, *East Tennessee and the Civil War*, written several years after the war, Heiskell, along with Swan, is depicted as ultraextremist "in their condemnation of Union people."[36] Temple claimed that Confederate authorities repeatedly sought information and advice from both men regarding the handling of the "unionist problem." In fact, by war's end, most Unionists probably considered Heiskell the most despised and hated secessionist in east Tennessee; he was personally accused of several atrocities and raids against Loyalist people not only in his home county of Hawkins but also in several nearby counties.[37] Later, in October 1861, Attorney Joseph Brown Heiskell would announce his candidacy for office to the Confederate Congress.[38]

Of the remaining attorneys in this initial group, only John Baxter, if called upon, could come close to providing a strong defense for Loyalists. Baxter, a strong Union man before the war, soon changed his stance after Tennessee seceded; he became a neutralist once it became clear to him the hopelessness of fighting against Confederates. Once the district court opened in September, Baxter voluntarily took the oath of allegiance to the Confederate States, in part so he could defend Unionists brought before the courts. Later that fall and winter of 1861–1862, Baxter used his influence in Richmond to gain the release of Unionist William G. Brownlow from a Knoxville prison cell.[39]

With most facing treason charges, the East Tennessee Confederate District Court paraded one-hundred-plus prisoners from the crackdown on disloyalty into court over a three-week span, beginning that second week of September. During the court session on Thursday, September 12, a group of twenty-one men made appearances before Judge Humphreys on charges of treason. All in this group appear to be residents of either Hawkins or Hancock County, Tennessee. Unfortunately, no county references directly connecting the various men were included in the court minutes. Also, the court record in only a few instances specified the first name of a defendant, while almost exclusively using or recording initials for first and middle names of defendants. Of course, this made identifications difficult at best, leaving some possibly open to question and doubt.

To overcome this failing, effort was made to utilize 1860 census records and military records where available, in order to improve the accuracy of identifications. Furthermore, if Confederates carried out the arrest after the bridge burnings in early November 1861, Knoxville jail records from the late 1861–early 1862 period, stored at the National Archives, supplemented the census and military records, thereby improving the overall accuracy of defendant or prisoner identifications. As a result of using the above records and our best efforts, the following men from Hawkins and Hancock Counties were identified as appearing before the court on that Thursday, September 12, 1861.[40]

Hancock County Residents

John McGhee   Identified as John McGee, age twenty-four, farm laborer, Levicy District of Hancock, living in the War Gap area of Hawkins County. Enlisted on July 10, 1862, Company A, First Tennessee Cavalry Regiment, USA.[41]

C.M. Trent   Identified as Curran M. Trent, age seventeen, farm laborer, War Creek, Hancock. Enlisted initially on February 1, 1863, in Company A, First Tennessee Cavalry Regiment, USA. Also later served in Companies H and M. Brother to Freelin Trent.

W. Pratt   Identified as William Pratt, age nineteen, farmer, resident of Sneedville, Hancock. Enlisted on March 9, 1862, in Company A, First Tennessee Cavalry Regiment, USA.

J. Bird   Identified as one of three Byrd family members, either James A. Bird, Andrew "Jackson" (Bird/Byrd) or John S. Byrd. If Andrew, he was age twenty-six, went by his middle name of Jackson during this period and resided at War Creek, Hancock. If he was James A. Bird, he was age forty-two, resided in Lee Valley, Hawkins, and enlisted in Company F, Second Tennessee Infantry Regiment, USA. If he was John S. Byrd, son of James A. Bird, he served in his father's Company F until his death from measles in March 1863.

L. Viles — Identified as Levi Viles, age twenty-five, War Creek, Hancock, farmhand of Wm. Trent Sr., living next to Wm. Trent Jr., age twenty-nine. Viles was a personal friend of James A. Bird, according to Bird's pension papers. Viles later enlisted in Company F, Second Tennessee Infantry Regiment, USA.

F. Trent — Identified as Freelin Trent, age fifteen, farm laborer, War Creek, Hancock. Enlisted on March 9, 1862, in Company A, First Tennessee Cavalry Regiment, USA. He was the son of Mary Trent, living three doors from Jackson and Enoch Byrd and four doors from Campbell Trent.

W. Trent — Identified as William Trent Jr., age twenty-nine, farmer, War Creek, Hancock. He lived next to his father, Wm. Trent Sr. and farmhand Levi Viles.

A. Stubblefield — Identified as Alexander Stubblefield, age sixteen, farmhand, Sneedville, Hancock. Enlisted on July 4, 1862, in Company B, First Tennessee Cavalry Regiment, USA; later served in Company G.

J. Jackson — Identified as James Jackson, farmer, Sneedville, Hancock.

Hawkins County Residents

W. Byrd — Identified as either Captain Wm. K. Byrd Sr. or son Wm. E. Byrd. If neither, it may have been Captain Byrd's grandson, Wm. K. Byrd, son of James A Bird. In 1860, Captain Wm. K. Byrd, age fifty-eight, a farmer, lived at Lee Valley, Hawkins, with son Lias "Levi" Bird, and two doors from eldest son, James A. Bird, and grandson William K (William R. in 1860 census). Captain Byrd's son, Wm E. Byrd, age thirty-eight, was a Methodist clergyman who lived in War Creek, Hancock. Grandson Wm. K. Byrd served as a private in Company F, Second Tennessee Infantry, USA, and later as captain in Company H, Eighth Tennessee Infantry, USA.

J. Cobb   Identified as Jackson Cobb, age fourteen, Lee Valley, Hawkins, living with the Anderson Lawson family.

E.S. McGinnis   Identified as Edward S. (Scott) McGinnis, age twenty-four, school teacher, Lee Valley, Hawkins.

D. Butter   Identified as David Buttery, age eighteen, Lee Valley, Hawkins. He was the son of James Buttery, age forty-one, and a next-door neighbor to Lias "Levi", James A. and Captain Wm. K. Byrd. David's father, James, was later arrested in December 1861 and sent to prison at Tuscaloosa, Alabama.

In summary, most of those arrested in this group lived either in Lee Valley, Hawkins County, or War Creek (Holland District), Hancock County—both areas where Unionist Byrd family members were known to have resided; also, as many as six of these men may have later served in the First Tennessee Cavalry Regiment, USA.[42] Furthermore, two of them are known to have been personal friends with James A. Bird, with one later joined in marriage after the war to a niece of James. That being eighteen-year-old C.M., or "Curran," as he was called, who married Phebe Byrd, daughter of James's brother, William E. Byrd. Both of these men, Curran M. Trent and Levi Viles, are found providing post–Civil War pension affidavits for James A. Bird. In fact, Levi Viles, age twenty-six, is noted in James's pension records as being a longtime friend for nearly thirty years. Viles further stated in one pension document that Bird recruited him to join Company F, Second Tennessee Infantry, USA. Of course, Viles and Trent lived in the apparent Unionist area of War Creek or Holland District of Hancock County.[43]

As far as the two men listed as J. Bird and W. Byrd, it's believed they are none other than James A. Bird and his father, Captain William K. Byrd, but further evidence is necessary before this can be fully confirmed. Also, it should be noted that both James and his father may have spelled their surname Bird; in fact, James's pension papers attest to this fact in the many affidavits submitted by friends, family and those with whom he served in the Union army. The vast majority used the "Bird" spelling, as well as James himself, who cosigned many of those same documents.

The hearing before Judge Humphreys concluded that day, with each man giving the Confederate oath of allegiance, thereby acknowledging himself "to be indebted to the Confederate States of America in the sum of one

Captain Lewis M. Jarvis, Company E, Eighth Tennessee Cavalry, USA, was a Hancock County man and possible relative of Loyalist and militia captain Joel W. Jarvis. Lewis Jarvis worked in civil service before the war. *Courtesy of Tennessee State Museum*

hundred dollars, yet to be void on condition that he should be a true and loyal citizen and subject to the laws of the state of Tennessee and of the Confederate States of America." In addition, each man promised "not to aid or assist the enemies" of the CSA or "engage in treasonable or rebellious plots or conspiracies," and should they "know of any plots or conspiracies being made or intended" they "would immediately inform the Legislative, Executive or Judicial authorities of the state of Tennessee or CSA." Afterward, each was required to pay court cost before being discharged.[44]

In a second court action on September 12, 1861, the two Hancock County Union activists, Joel Jarvis and C.L. Barton, both arrested in August, came before the court. According to the *Knoxville Register*, a prosecessionist daily, it stated Barton had represented Hancock County at the Greeneville Union convention back in June, while Jarvis captained a Unionist home guard company in Hancock County. Jarvis, a Virginian by birth, resided in the Davis District of Hancock, with its post office at Sneedville.[45] Barton, identified as Charles L. Barton, originally from Illinois, would later serve as captain in the First Tennessee Cavalry Regiment, USA.[46] Also, Joel Jarvis is believed to have been a brother, or at least a close relative, of Captain Lewis (Louis) M. Jarvis, also born in Virginia, who served in Company E,

Eighth Tennessee Cavalry Regiment, USA, a unit formed in Sneedville in the summer of 1863, consisting of Hancock County men.[47]

The *Knoxville Register* article recounted that, soon after the Greeneville convention, both Joel Jarvis and Charles Barton left for Kentucky to consult with "the minions of Lincoln and his man Friday, Andy Johnson, as to the means of invading East Tennessee with a northern army." Upon returning to Hancock County area, the two men recruited about twenty-five others to join their company. Soon afterward, Jarvis and Barton attempted to leave again for Kentucky with their newly formed company only to be arrested while crossing the mountains.[48]

Pleading not guilty to treason charges in their district court appearance, Barton and Jarvis were turned over to custody of military officer Brigadier General Felix Zollicoffer with orders to convey both to the marshal in Nashville to answer other possible charges on the fourth Monday of October 1861. Along with Barton and Jarvis, two other Hancock County men, John McGhee and Curran M. Trent along with H.M. Johnson, defendants in the first action, were ordered by the court to appear in Nashville as possible witnesses in the Barton and Jarvis action. Interestingly, a few days later, after being released to military authorities for transport, Barton and Jarvis were placed with three other prisoners—presumably McGhee, Trent and Johnson—aboard the train to Nashville under escort of Confederate soldiers commanded by Captain Henry M. Ashby. Near Wartrace, Barton received permission to go to the "water closet" to satisfy his thirst. But taking a little too long to get his drink, a suspicious Rebel soldier opened the door to discover that Barton had jumped from the moving train through a window. Authorities immediately halted the train, where a hurried search ensued to recapture Barton but to no avail.[49] Because of this daring escape from Rebels and other similar exploits supposedly attributed to him, Barton gained a certain amount of notoriety and fame among Unionists. Surviving those early exploits, Barton later accepted an officer's position in the First Tennessee Infantry Regiment, USA. In fact, there is evidence Barton may have served in at least one or two other Union military units in addition to the First Tennessee Infantry.

Other persons arrested during the September term of the district court included several notables, such as local Knoxvillians John Bell Brownlow, son of William G. "Parson" Brownlow, and local merchant Perez Dickinson. John Bell ultimately spent several nights in jail but later was released; Dickinson, arrested in response to the Alien Enemies Act, eventually posted bond to ensure his good behavior and freedom. Another arrest involved

John Bell Brownlow, son of Parson Brownlow, was arrested on what amounted to trumped-up charges, supposedly for circulating "treasonous and incendiary" material. *Courtesy of Tennessee State Museum.*

notable Dr. John W. Thornburgh of Union County, accused of leading a home guard, or Union militia. Dr. Thornburgh, or Captain Thornburgh, as addressed by the court, faced court accusations of "traitorously assembling men together armed with guns, lances and home made bowie knifes to give aid and comfort to the people and to levy war in favor of the United States." Thornburgh's court hearing resulted in him being sent to Nashville and imprisoned for a period of time before gaining his release.[50]

On September 21, 1861, William G. Brownlow, after several weeks of self-restraint and conciliatory posture, spoke out from his Unionist *Knoxville Whig* newspaper in an article titled "Indiscriminate Arrests," stating that Union men were being arrested without proper cause. He went as far as to quote Judge Humphreys of the district court, who pronounced earlier that same day in open court a "Stern rebuke (of) the spirit of some small men about this town, in causing indiscriminate arrests and for insufficient causes."

According to Brownlow, this stinging rebuke by the judge only angered secessionists who had pushed for the stronger policies against Tories. Making still further claims, Brownlow accused Confederate authorities of arresting Loyalist men "on account of old political and personal quarrels… or for having dared to vote against" secessionism. Of the sixty to seventy men arrested, Brownlow claimed only about ten "could be considered as having committed any offense against the peace and dignity of the State or Confederate government." If the arrests continued, Brownlow foresaw only further damage and alienation between Loyalist and Southern supporters, serving only "to gratify the bad feeling of bad men."[51]

The *Athens Post* of McMinn County, a secessionist newspaper, editorialized on October 3 that too much emphasis was being placed by Confederate authorities on arresting and trying Unionist "dupes" rather than the "big men" and "deceivers." The newspaper elaborated in a strongly worded statement, saying, "When the serpents head is off, he is powerless for harm."

The article, written in response to recent arrests and district court trials of twenty-four Unionists from McMinn County, attempted to show the sheer inability of Confederate authorities, including the district court, to adequately deal with the Unionist problem. Complaining further, the writer noted the court's only requirements for the twenty-four arrested amounted to taking the oath of allegiance or giving personal recognizance.[52]

The first session of the Confederate district court ended on September 25, surprisingly without District Attorney John Crozier Ramsey getting one conviction. This result was largely due to Judge Humphreys refusal to find many of the activities Unionists were involved in as being treasonous. Of the one hundred men or so tried during this court term, only two local Knoxville citizens had been arrested, with the court's primary focus being those arrested and brought in from outlying counties, such as Hawkins, Hancock, Union and Jefferson Counties. The majority ultimately took the Confederate oath of allegiance, agreeing to pay a future fine to obtain their release and ensure their loyalty, thereby avoiding harsher treatment.[53]

But Parson Brownlow continued to complain well into mid-October about the continuation of "malicious arrests" of Unionists; in reality, only a few like Jarvis, Barton and Thornburgh had actually been bound over by the court to military authorities for transport to Nashville and future trials. Even so, the events of September, as mild as they may have seemed for some, became the opening act in a increasing wave of harsh treatment against Union people and was soon to pale in comparison to what Confederates would unleash after the events of November 8, 1861.

CHAPTER 3
The Bridge Burnings

O n the night of November 8, 1861, several parties of Union men carried out the first phase of a plan formulated and promoted by William Blount Carter.[54] Some historians credit William G. "Parson" Brownlow as actually conceiving the plan, but evidence supporting such a conclusion is inconsistent. The plan entailed the simultaneous burning of nine important bridges on the East Tennessee–Georgia and East Tennessee–Virginia Railroads between Bridgeport, Alabama, and Bristol, Tennessee. With destruction of the bridge at Bridgeport over the Tennessee River, the Memphis-Charleston Railroad would be prevented from connecting with the Western-Atlantic, the main supply line from Memphis and Nashville to Richmond.[55] This covert operation had the financial backing of the Federal government and strong support of Union general George McClellan and President Abraham Lincoln.

Having heard the cries for help from east Tennessee Unionists, Lincoln for weeks repeatedly urged his generals to occupy east Tennessee at the earliest possible time. He felt deep concern for the welfare of the Union people of east Tennessee and knew of the strong Union sentiment dividing east Tennessee from the rest of the state. Just as important, Lincoln knew that east Tennessee had strategic importance to both the Union and Confederacy. For the South, the railroads crisscrossing east Tennessee and connecting critical points in the lower South to Virginia and other points east were absolutely vital to the long-term survival of the Confederacy. For the North, east Tennessee offered a tremendous potential for recruiting and a prospect

President Abraham Lincoln early on considered east Tennessee and support of local Unionist critical, but he had trouble convincing his generals. *Courtesy of Library of Congress.*

for statehood, if only Union forces could find a way to take control of the area and begin organizing. Carter's plan offered a chance for accomplishing those important Union goals.[56]

The second phase of Carter's plan involved a military objective, with its goal being the invasion of Tennessee by Union soldiers from Kentucky and the capture of the town of Knoxville. If successful, the railroad communication through east Tennessee, between Richmond and the southwestern part of the Confederacy, would be cut or severely disrupted.[57] This part of the plan was

 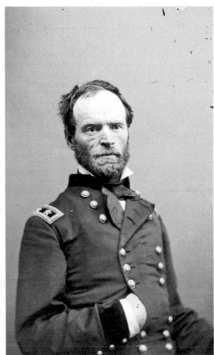

Left: Major General George H. Thomas, unlike other senior Union officers, supported William B. Carter's invasion and bridge burning plan. *Courtesy of Library of Congress.*

Right: Major General William T. Sherman had serious doubts about the Carter plan, no doubt due in part to his impaired judgment resulting from an unstable emotional state at the time. *Courtesy of Library of Congress.*

originally slated to coincide closely with the bridge burnings. Union generals George Thomas and Samuel P. Carter received permission from General William T. Sherman to execute the military phase of Carter's plan. The loyal Second Tennessee Infantry Regiment, recently formed in Kentucky and lead by Carter, became an important part of the scheme. Breaking camp on October 18, 1861, General Carter's loyal Tennessee regiments and General Thomas's Indiana and Ohio regiments headed toward Cumberland Gap to execute the invasion. Along the way, they skirmished with Confederate forces under the command of General Felix Zollicoffer at Wildcat, Kentucky. But upon arriving at London, Kentucky, on October 28, they received a new order from General Sherman, halting their advance and effectively aborting the invasion.

Despite having President Lincoln and General McClellan's approval, Sherman reluctantly agreed to go along with the scheme initially, but now with his latest order, he reversed his decision and decided the Union troops lacked sufficient training, and their numbers were too few to overcome the more experienced and larger Confederate forces concentrated in the area.[58] When informed of Sherman's order halting the invasion, Carter's troops threw down their rifles in disgust and many left. Some pleaded, some wept and some shouted angry words against Sherman for halting their return to their families and native east Tennessee.[59]

Thus, with this second phase or military invasion postponed indefinitely, the bridges burners who had left Camp Dick Robinson just ahead of the military for Tennessee were now on their own, with no apparent knowledge that the second phase of their operation had been canceled. This failure by the military would become a major problem for the Union people of east Tennessee. With the ensuing bridge attacks just days away and no military protection forthcoming, the Union people would soon find themselves in grave danger, left alone to face the full force of Rebel vengeance and retribution.[60]

Regardless of the aborted military action, the bridge attacks took place as planned under the cover of darkness on November 8, 1861. While not all successful, the attacks created great excitement and alarm all over Tennessee and the South. Unionists either partially or totally destroyed five of the nine wooden railroad bridges planned for destruction, while failing to take out the other four due to the bridge either being heavily guarded or the attack being botched. These attacks, the first overt acts of resistance in Tennessee from among the people under Confederate power, amounted to a serious act of war—not simple mischief or vandalism—but for the purpose of disrupting military operations of the Confederacy.[61] But probably more significant than the attacks, the bridge burnings had a startling psychological impact. The Confederate government assumed immediately that the attacks signaled a revolt among Union people all over east Tennessee, with an invasion of Union soldiers from Kentucky soon forthcoming.[62] The Confederate government immediately placed authorities on high alert. Word of the burnings spread like wildfire, quickly from town to town, creating panic, fear and much uncertainty among citizens and Confederate authorities.

Adding to this elevated panic and excitement came other reports flowing into Confederate authorities and military leaders, indicating that Union men all over east Tennessee were forming in large groups and threatening new attacks, with one group estimated as large as 1,500 men. The truth of the matter is, while some of these reports contained some sincerity and accuracy, many more were exaggerated in their numbers and descriptions of the actual threat, serving only to fuel more panic and fear.[63]

Within days, on November 12, a very concerned Tennessee governor, Isham Harris, wrote President Jefferson Davis from Nashville:

> *The burning of the railroad bridges in East Tennessee shows deep-seated spirit of rebellion in that section. Union men are organizing. The rebellion must be crushed out instantly, the leaders arrested and summarily punished. I shall send immediately about 10 thousand men to that section. If you can possibly send from Western Virginia a number of Tennessee regiments to East Tennessee, we can repair the bridges and crush the rebellion.*

About this same time, other dispatches sent to Confederate regiments ordered units "to commence simultaneously disarming Union inhabitants" and seize and hold their leaders as prisoners.

On November 25, J.P. Benjamin, Confederate secretary of war, wrote the following instructions to Confederate colonel W.B. Wood, at Knoxville: "All such as can be identified as having been engaged in bridge burning are to be tried summarily by drum-head court-martial, and if found guilty, executed on the spot by hanging." Wood at the time was acting post commander during General Zollicoffer's absence.

Benjamin went on to say in the same dispatch that "all such as have not been so engaged are to be treated as prisoners of war, and sent with an armed guard to Tuscaloosa, Alabama, there to be kept imprisoned," and if "you can discover that arms are concealed by these traitors, you will send out detachments, search for and size the arms."

Benjamin closed his dispatch by saying that in "no case should any of these men, if known to have been up in arms against the government be release on any oath or pledge of allegiance, the time for such measures is past."[64]

On November 30, 1861, from his Knoxville headquarters, Confederate colonel Danville Leadbetter, in an effort to quell Unionists and control the unrest in his jurisdiction, put forth a "proclamation to the citizens of East Tennessee."[65] Leadbetter, an engineer, had been assigned a troop commanded by Secretary Benjamin soon after the attacks and given responsibility for rebuilding and guarding the bridges between Bristol and Chattanooga, Tennessee, and keeping lines of communication open.

In his notice, Leadbetter noted, "So long as the question of Union or Disunion was debatable," it was permissible to do so until the vote. But once the people approved secession, "you did ill to distract the country by angry words and insurrectionary tumult."

Leadbetter went on to claim that east Tennesseans should expect to enjoy prosperity and happiness under the Confederacy because "every product of your agriculture and workshops will now find a prompt sale at high prices."

But Leadbetter goes on to warn, "So long as you are up in arms against these States, can you look for any thing but invasion of your homes, and the wasting away of your substance. The government commands the peace and sends troops enough to enforce the order."

He also goes on to "lay out the olive branch to unionist" by stating, "Every man who comes in promptly and delivers up his arms will be pardoned on taking the oath of allegiance."

But closing his proclamation, Leadbetter offered his severest warning:

> *All men taken in arms against the government will be transported to the military prison at Tuscaloosa…and all bridge burners and destroyers of railroad track are excepted from among those pardonable. They will be tried by drum head court martial and be hanged on the spot.*

On the same day as his proclamation message to the people, Leadbetter seemed to put an exclamation point to his announcement by keeping his word and hanging two Unionists for bridge burning: Henry Fry and Jacob M. Hensie, more recently identified as Jacob Madison "Matt" Hinshaw. Both were hanged in a tree near the old depot in Greeneville, Tennessee, where their bodies reportedly stayed on public display "for 26 hours before anyone was allowed to cut them down."[66]

Thus began the "reign of the rebels," as some have called this period in east Tennessee history. This intense activity of arrest and imprisonment of Union people by Confederate authorities and sympathizers, more widespread and severe than the previous summer and fall, lasted well into the following year of 1862. With these latest events, no sympathetic judge or conciliatory policy by a leading Confederate military figure could shield Unionists from the animosity and hatred now directed their way. After the bridge burnings, many Confederate officials concluded that General Felix Zollicoffer's conciliatory policies with Unionists in the fall had been a complete failure. In fact, after the bridge burnings, Zollicoffer himself felt betrayed by Unionists and believed that stronger measures were now necessary.[67]

Actions taken by Confederate authorities after the bridge burning wrote a new, infamous chapter in their effort to suppress Unionism in east Tennessee, one marked by hundreds of arrests, imprisonments and deaths. One writer has estimated that between 2,500 and 3,000 Union people or supporters lost their lives in east Tennessee during this period.[68] Among the hundreds of arrests, only five of the bridge burners suffered the death penalty for their crimes, while four others connected with the scheme eventually went to prison.

Perhaps more important and devastating, the policies put in place by J.P. Benjamin and Confederate military leaders after November 8 had the effect of creating roving bands of agents, in the form of Confederate military companies and civilian sympathizers or home guard units, that scattered out all over east Tennessee. The chief goal among these roving bands or loose military units was the suppression of any resistance by Unionists, whether overt or suspected, to Confederate authority, regardless of the suffering or ruin caused by their actions. Throughout the war, these guard units or civilian sympathizer groups, both Unionist and secessionist alike, routinely operated outside the law and beyond the control of established military. In such an environment, competing groups quickly became judge and juries, which in turn spawned and provoked many of the atrocities committed during the war and for several years thereafter.

What follows is the story of one of those three thousand Union people, who with his family and a few brave men stood their ground against this onslaught of terror, arrest and imprisonment. This is the story of Captain William K. Byrd, a Union man from Hawkins County, Tennessee, who paid the ultimate price for his loyalty and love of country.

CHAPTER 4

They "Drew the Vengeance of the Rebels"

On Sunday, November 24, 1861, Eliza Fain records a revealing entry in her diary regarding her son, Isaac "Ike" Fain, leaving for Bays Mountain, southeast of Rogersville, with a gun strapped to his back, where "a number of Union men have collected for resistance to the law."[69] Four days later, in a W.L. Dickson letter dated November 28 from Mooresburg, Hawkins County, Dickson mentioned a "regiment of soldiers" arriving in Rogersville from Knoxville a few days prior, for the purpose of protecting "Rogersville and the adjoining country from a band of Lincolnites that had collected;" further evidence of continued Unionist activity in the surrounding area.

Sometime during the fall of 1861, William K. Byrd, about age sixty-two, living in the Lee Valley area of Hawkins County (according to the 1860 census), assumed leadership as captain of a Union militia made up of men from Hancock and Hawkins Counties. According to his oldest son's Civil War pension papers, William K. Byrd and his sons committed very early to the Union cause. One son, Ephraim Byrd, age twenty-eight and second youngest, apparently made a decision to serve in his father's militia. Eldest son James Anderson Bird, a farmer and part-time parson living near his father in Lee Valley and possessing strong views regarding the Union, often traveled about the area, giving patriotic Union speeches. In James's pension papers, one affidavit described James as an "earnest Union man, one of the first to leave for Kentucky for Union military service in 1861," joining up as a second lieutenant with Company F, Second Tennessee Infantry, USA.

Upon returning later that year to the Hancock-Hawkins County area, James recruited others to join the Union army. Two of those recruits were his two eldest sons, William K. and John S. Byrd.[70]

Two other sons of the elder William K. Byrd later committed as well to the Union cause. Levi Benjamin Bird, age twenty-four, enlisted in September 1863, serving until the end of the war with Company E, Eighth Tennessee Cavalry Regiment, USA.[71] Son William E. Byrd, age thirty-nine, is believed to have served with the same company as Levi, with some evidence purporting his capture at the Wyerman Mill battle in Lee County, Virginia, on February 22, 1864.[72] In further regard to William, there is evidence from the Civil War pension papers of Larkin Stapleton, who lived in the Lee Valley area of Hawkins County, which indicated that William E. Byrd operated as guide or pilot in the spring of 1862 for Union men seeking to steal away to Kentucky. According to Stapleton, on one particular instance Byrd attempted to lead Stapleton and a company of fifty to sixty Union men to Kentucky to join the Union army, but Confederates captured most of the contingent only a day or two out, just south of the Powell River. This resulted in Stapleton and an unknown number being sent to prison at Madison, Georgia, for two months. Unfortunately, the full extent of William E. Byrd's activities as pilot for Union recruits before and after this incident remains unknown.[73]

Ultimately, these various Union activities by the Byrds leading up to the fall of 1861 "drew the vengeance of the rebels upon him [James] and his family."[74] Even so, if the Byrds feared possible Rebel vengeance or reprisals, it doesn't seem to have deterred them and other Unionists from organizing in response to the growing "reign of terror," now underway by marauding Confederate groups since the bridge burnings. But by the end of November 1861, open resistance by any person or group to Confederate rule had become unwise and dangerous. By then, Confederate authorities were viewing almost any public or personal displays of Union support as treasonous behavior, worthy of either arrest and imprisonment or possible death, depending upon circumstances.

So to neutralize this Unionist threat in surrounding Hancock–northern Hawkins County area, the Confederates and secessionists responded by sending a newly organized company and at least one fully mustered military unit against Byrd's militia and other Lincolnists.[75] The main Confederate force consisted of men associated with Company E, Forty-third Tennessee Infantry, CSA, at the time a nonmustered unit organized in Rogersville less than a month before the raid and supplemented with a sizeable group of civilian Confederate sympathizers from the same area.[76] It's believed the

Confederate sympathizers and E Company acted as a combined force during the raid.[77] In fact, significant evidence characterizes this combined force as a guerrilla or marauder group more interested in exerting force and control than self-defense. In addition, along with the involvement of E Company, a second Confederate military company may have participated in the Byrd raid as well—a fully mustered unit known as Company D, Fourth (Branner's) Tennessee Cavalry Battalion, CSA.[78]

Control of these various groups rested with at least two men and maybe as many as five. Leadership of the first group, or Company E, Forty-third Tennessee Infantry, CSA, resided with Captain John W. Phillips and First Lieutenant Joseph Huffmaster.[79] Leadership of the civilian Confederate sympathizers included possibly two men, the first being a man named Bynum, thought to be John Gray Bynum,[80] and Joseph Brown Heiskell, newly elected Confederate congressman. In fact, Heiskell, or "Colonel" Heiskell as friends, acquaintances and other secessionists often addressed him during this period, may have had sole leadership of the raiding party on the day in question.

The third group, or Company D of Branner's battalion, operated under the command of a "Captain Simpson," believed to be Robert Simpson. Simpson's company organized in Rogersville, Hawkins County, the previous July and apparently acted in a support or follow-up role, handling transport and disposition of prisoners taken in the raid. A letter dated December 10, 1861, and written by W.L. Dickson from Mooresburg, Hawkins County, to his sister, seems to confirm as much regarding Captain Simpson's company. In the letter, Dickson mentioned Simpson's company as having been stationed about three hundred miles from here at Monticello, Kentucky; in the same breath, he describes the fight with Byrd's militia, the killing of Captain Byrd and the capture of Byrd's son and several others. Furthermore, Dickson noted prisoners from the fight, including Byrd's son, as being held temporarily overnight in Mooresburg by soldiers, presumedly from Simpson's company, and apparently destined for Knoxville. On the contrary, the official record fails to mention Simpson's company (at the time organizationally part of Branner's battalion as previously noted) by name or its activities during this period or after its muster on October 4, 1861 at Camp Buckner near Cumberland Ford, or Pineville, Kentucky. But military records do confirm the presence of unnamed units of Branner's battalion in the vicinity of Monticello about the third week in November 1861, offering some support for Simpson's location implied by Dickson, roughly two weeks ahead of the raid on Byrd's militia.

But more revealing is a personal account of Wylie Miller Young, written by his cousin, DeWolfe Miller. Both Young and Miller served at different times in Simpson's D Company, with Young enlisting on August 1, 1861, at Cumberland Ford, Kentucky, and Miller on February 1, 1864, at Rogersville. Young, who served nearly a year in Simpson's D Company, indicated the unit after its organization at Rogersville and a brief period at Knoxville, "marched on to Powell's Valley at Lafollette [Tennessee]," a location approximately sixty-five to seventy miles from the town of Sneedville, Hancock County. Powell's Valley is formed by the Powell River as it flows out of Virginia into Hancock County, Tennessee, from northeast to the southwest. Young stated D Company, once arriving, "soldiered up and down the valley until going into Kentucky with Felix Zollicoffer—(where they) fought the battle of Wildcat, thence [afterward] back to Powell's Valley."

The battle of Wildcat Mountain took place on October 21, 1861, in Laurel County, Kentucky, just a few miles northwest of the town of London. After returning to Powell's Valley, Simpson's D Company apparently remained in the area until, as Young noted, returning to Kentucky near the end of December or early January 1862 to rejoin Zollicoffer in the battle of Mill Springs on January 19, 1862.[81]

In summary, if as it appears, Simpson's D Company was in Powell's Valley from approximately November 1 to possibly December 31, 1861; that means they could have been as close as only a few miles, up to seventy miles from Sneedville, and therefore not too distant from either the town or the suspected location of the skirmish with Byrd's militia. If this analysis is correct, Simpson's company could have played a far greater role in the confrontation with Byrd than first suspected. At any rate, establishing Captain Simpson and his company's exact location just prior to the Byrd raid and its degree of involvement will probably forever remain a point of conjecture.

As far as E Company, the other Confederate unit connected to the Byrd raid, there is no doubt concerning its involvement; substantiating evidence uncovered from several sources supports this conclusion. Organized in Rogersville, Tennessee, on November 5, 1861, E Company was fully mustered six weeks later on December 14, 1861, at Knoxville, along with nine other companies, comprising the original Forty-third Infantry Regiment, CSA.

But surprisingly, after its muster in mid-December, Confederate secretary of war J.P. Benjamin several weeks later nearly mustered the unit out for "lack of arms."[82] Despite this acknowledged weapons shortage by the Forty-third Infantry Regiment, it's felt that Captain John W. Phillips's E

Company was the unnamed unit that came up from Knoxville to protect the Hawkins area, which Dickson noted in his letter of November 28, 1861. The Forty-third, or elements of this regiment, are recorded as being stationed at Knoxville during this period, from November 5 to December 31, 1861, and E Company, consisting mostly of Hawkins County men, with other members of the Forty-third, could have eagerly made the trip back to Rogersville to protect families and friends from the growing Lincolnite threat in the surrounding area.

Along with the above two military units, the civilian group of Confederate sympathizers may have been the largest of the three groups supporting the raid. It appears at least twenty-five to thirty men or more in this group included many of the same men listed in a grand jury indictment for the murder of Captain William K. Byrd, issued in October 1865 in Hawkins County.[83] Most of those men in the murder indictment lacked any membership in any organized military unit at the time of the raid, which provided some justification for including them with Bynum's group.

Events in and around Hawkins and Hancock Counties by the first week of December 1861 clearly had both sides on a collision course. Confederate authorities still reeled from the bridge burnings the previous month and seemed void of any feelings or thoughts of compromise. In fact, they had long since lost patience with Unionists and the belief that Unionists "would eventually see the light" and submit to the new Southern government. Unionists, on the other hand, continued to organize and flex their muscles while still believing in a soon-coming Union military invasion of east Tennessee from Kentucky, the same invasion some had expected immediately after the bridge burnings. So as this standoff continued, and as November turned in December, it became obvious neither side in the Hancock-Hawkins area intended to back down. With direct confrontation no longer in doubt, only the time and place remained unknown. This volatile situation, a virtual smoldering powder keg, burst into flames near Clinch Mountain on Saturday, December 7, 1861.

CHAPTER 5

Confrontation: The Byrd Raid

During that first week of December 1861, the weather turned cold in the Hawkins County area, with a hard freeze recorded on Tuesday, December 3; skies remained mostly sunny.[84] More importantly, the situation on Clinch—seemingly unaffected by the cool weather—continued to grow in intensity, as demonstrated in a comment from the diary of Eliza Rhea Anderson Fain on Thursday December 5: "George Powel and Joseph Huffmaster brought home Buck Huffmaster, who was shot in going from camp to Sneedville [Hancock County]."[85]

This important detail showed limited fighting, or bushwhacking, between Unionists and Confederates was well underway in the Sneedville area of Hancock County area during the first week of December 1861. Also, the presence of Joseph Huffmaster, a first lieutenant in the newly organized Company E, Forty-third Tennessee Infantry, further established the presence of that unit or members of it in the northern Hawkins-Hancock County area just two days before the Byrd raid. Furthermore, from Eliza's comment, it appears that they had been in the area more than a few days, certainly long enough to establish an encampment.

The next evening, on December 6, the night before the raid, Eliza wrote again in her diary: "My sons Samuel Gammon and Ike are both across the mountains not many miles distant from home."[86]

Of course, like First Lieutenant Huffmaster, both Samuel and Ike were documented members of Company E. Thus, with Huffmaster having brought home the wounded from the Sneedville or Hancock County area the day before, its appears Eliza's reference to Samuel and Ike being "across the mountains" is another clear reference to Clinch Mountain and the Sneedville area of Hancock County.

On Saturday, December 7, 1861, the situation, according to Hancock County court records, erupted into a deadly confrontation near the Hancock-Hawkins County line between Byrd's Union, or Lincolnist, militia and the combined force of Confederate military and secessionist sympathizers. Other than Eliza's account placing it on a "high spur of that mountain region," the exact location and time of the fight is currently unknown. With Eliza's references to Sneedville and other commentary, it's our belief that the locale is either in Lee Valley, Hawkins County area, or on War Ridge or Pine Ridge near "Pumpkin Valley," both areas lying north of Clinch Mountain in far northern Hawkins County, and near or just over the Hancock County line. Supporting this belief, and according to the 1860 census, William K. Byrd Sr., with sons James Anderson Bird and Levi, lived in Lee Valley,[87] while sons Ephraim "Enoch," William E. and Andrew Jackson resided in the Holland District or War Creek area of Hancock County.[88] In fact, Pine Ridge and War Ridge are areas where various Byrd family members have lived for many years, before and after the Civil War, up until the early 1900s.

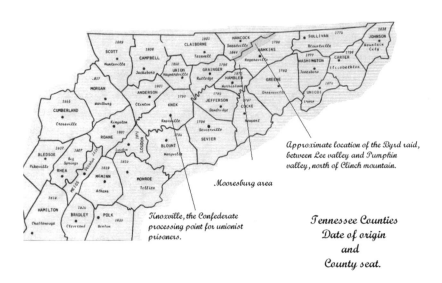

Approximate location of the Byrd raid, between Lee valley and Pumpkin valley, north of Clinch mountain.

Mooresburg area

Knoxville, the Confederate processing point for unionist prisoners.

Tennessee Counties Date of origin and County seat.

East Tennessee map. *Courtesy of the author's collection.*

Confrontation: The Byrd Raid

Specific details of actual fighting are few, but Eliza recorded in her diary that Buck Huffmaster and son Ike made a narrow escape from the skirmish with Byrd's militia. Young Ike afterward told his mother of never feeling "so frightened in his life, with bullets flying by him and not being able to see," no doubt due to the smoke of discharging firearms and the sheer fear of a young recruit. Once the skirmish ended, Byrd's militia and other Lincolnists had suffered a defeat by Confederates, forcing them to scatter and flee for safety. Also important, the Confederate raiding party had captured four or five Unionists, including a wounded Captain Byrd. After disarming Byrd, the Rebel captors left him on the battlefield, while they sought assistance "to bring him down." Now alone and possibly bleeding from his wounds, Captain Byrd attempted to escape by hiding in the cover of a fallen tree some 150 to 200 yards away from the battlefield, staying hidden for nearly four hours before being discovered by returning Rebels. By then, a weakened Byrd, unable to stand on his own power and suffering greatly from his wounds and likely loss of blood, was overwhelmed and dragged from his concealment. Shortly thereafter, Byrd's captors placed him against a tree stump and summarily executed him by firearms.

Supporting the above scenario are at least three accounts of the wounding and killing of Byrd, including one by Eliza. As expected, of course, Eliza's account depicted the skirmish from a Confederate perspective in a diary entry dated December 26, 1861. Referring to this entry, Eliza noted, "Ole man Bird, a man of 60 years was one of the leaders of the rebellion," and was "said to be a bold, daring and fearless man."

She also noted Byrd as having been "shot on a high spur of that mountain region, disarmed and left by the man who shot him, while he went for assistance to bring him down." While alone, "the old man crept off some 150 to 200 yards but is deterred from making his escape beyond the reach of his pursuers by his wounds."

Eliza goes on to acknowledge sorrow and regret at Byrd's death, stating this "poor old fellow, I have felt troubled when I thought of his death." She concluded by placing the blame for Byrd's death on the "leading Union men of East Tennessee, [there should] rest the blood of these poor deluded victims."[89]

Another account of the Byrd raid comes from Crawford W. Hall's rare book, *Threescore Years and Ten*, which offered more details of the fight and death of Byrd but from a Unionist perspective. Hall's version of the raid, while consistent with Eliza's version, stated, "Bird was wounded and his company was dispersed, leaving him on the battleground. He crawled into a fallen treetop, and was discovered by some rebels, who had volunteered to go upon the raid."

But Hall added that, after discovery, Byrd was "dragged from his hiding-place, and being unable to stand on account of his wounds, was set up against a stump and shot to death for the amusement of those patriotic volunteers in the cause of treason."[90]

Hall's version of Byrd's death by firearms is further supported by a document from a Hawkins County Circuit Court grand jury held in October 1865. It described in chilling detail Byrd's fatal wound, noting death by the "force of gun power shot...in and upon the breast of him the said William Bird...one mortal wound of a depth of 6 inches and of the breadth of one inch."[91]

Hall concluded Byrd's death made such a stir among Union people in east Tennessee that it resulted in similar Union militias being formed in Carter and Johnson Counties.

Casualty numbers from the fight, uncovered in the Hancock County Chancery Court records, while not detailed, noted four or five militiamen, or Lincolnists, killed from gunshot or possible hanging, while the number of wounded failed to be reflected.[92] Of the men killed in the raid, only the identities of William K. Byrd and possibly John Wiett (Wyatt?) are known at this time. On the other hand, John Wiett's reputed death by hanging, taken from the chancery court testimony of Hancock County resident Malon Anderson may lack validity due to the fact that Knoxville jail records suggest Wiett possibly survived the skirmish with Confederates, only to be later arrested and imprisoned at Knoxville.[93] The John Wiett as noted in the chancery record is believed to be John Wiatt, age fifty-one in census records, a distiller by trade who lived in the Davis District of Hancock County, next door to Unionist and militia leader Joel Jarvis. Of course, the East Tennessee District Court had arrested and hauled Jarvis, along with Charles Barton, into court on treason charges the previous September. As far as Confederate losses, no casualty numbers are known at this time, other than maybe Buck Huffmaster, who was wounded two days earlier.

More details regarding the raid are found in a second letter written by W.L. Dickson to his sister, dated December 10, 1861, from Mooresburg, Hawkins County. In this letter, Dickson related,

> *There was a gathering of Lincolnites in Hancock County a week or so ago, but soldiers went over there and attacked them and defeated them. Eight soldiers with four Lincolnite...prisoners staid [sic] all night with us last night. Capt. Simpson's company [having] been stationed about three hundred miles from here in Monticello in Kentucky. The commander of the*

Hancock Lincolnites was Mr. Bird, one of the prisoners here last night was his sone [sic] *Elihu* [sic]. *I think that they will hang him. His gun flashed twice in the fight.*[94]

In the Dickson letter, "Elihu," is believed to be Ephraim Byrd or Enoch Byrd, as noted in the 1860 Hawkins County census. Confederate authorities took Ephraim and the other men to Knoxville, and imprisoned them for several weeks, likely at the infamous Knoxville jail some called "Castle Fox."

One thing is certain: Confederates clearly sought to do more than just disarm and arrest Union men. From the loss of life, it's apparent the leaders and men of this raiding party intended on "sending a message," possibly by killing Byrd and as many of his militia and other Lincolnists while dealing harshly with prisoners. Recalling the words of J.P. Benjamin, Confederate secretary of war, only days before the raid, the time for leniency and oaths of allegiance from Union people had long since ended. The treasonous bridge attacks by Unionists the month before had forever changed any tenuous status quo existing prior to November 8, 1861. Now the full force of Rebel vengeance, every bit unrelenting and deadly, now weighed heavily upon Lincolnist men like Byrd's militia.

CHAPTER 6

The Arrests Begin

Within hours of the clash with Byrd's militia, Confederates spread into the surrounding Hancock and northern Hawkins area, arresting known Byrd militia members and other Union sympathizers, now hiding and fearing for their lives and reeling from defeat suffered the previous day. Using Knoxville jail records and the 1860 census, a list of arrestees and sequence of those apprehensions and other critical details are established.[95]

The first Unionists reported arrested were William L. Green, age thirty-six, a Baptist clergyman, and Joseph Green, age sixteen, the apparent young son of James Green, who lived in the War Creek area of Hancock County within short distances of Captain Byrd's two sons and other known Unionists. Taken into custody on Sunday, a day after the raid, the Greens' jail records accused them of attempting to leave for "Kentucky for arms and men" and noted both as being arrested by a "Serg't Inman." In fact, those same Knoxville jail records noted several arrests in Hawkins and Hancock Counties by the same officer during December 1861, but unfortunately his unit name isn't recorded.[96] A review of military rosters of both units suspected of participating in the Byrd raid— Company E, Forty-third Tennessee Infantry and Company D, Fourth (Branner's) Tennessee Cavalry Battalion—failed to reveal any member having a surname of "Inman." Nonetheless, after examining other information, including census and Hancock County Chancery Court records, it's felt that "Serg't. Inman" might in fact be Lieutenant Larkin W. Eidson, age thirty-one, a member of E Company, Forty-third Infantry the day of the raid.

Larkin enlisted as a lieutenant on November 5, 1861, and was implicated after the war via court testimony by Andrew Jackson Byrd as "leading the raid" the day Andrew's father died—a significant fact in itself. According to official Tennessee Civil War service records, Larkin never achieved a rank beyond second lieutenant, but another source indicates him being elected as a first lieutenant in E Company in May 1862, which may relate to one jail entry identifying "Serge's Inman" as "Lieut. Inman." Furthermore, the 1860 census listed Larkin W. Eidson as "L.W. Itson" of War Gap, Hawkins County.[97] This simple discrepancy or apparent confusion regarding the spelling of the "Eidson" name does create some doubt as to the exact pronunciation, especially when considering this time period when illiteracy was much more widespread. That being said, it seems both possible and reasonable for someone to construe either "Eidson" or "Itson" as being "Inman." On the other hand, this incorrect census spelling may have resulted solely from the sloppy work of the local and likely semi-illiterate census taker, who merely recorded what they heard, without conscious effort to alter any pronunciation or spelling.

One other possible identification for the mysterious "Serg't Inman," one more likely than Eidson, is a man by the name of Samuel C. Inman, who was a cousin to Miss Myra Inman, a young teenage girl who lived in the Cleveland, Tennessee area, who kept a diary from 1859 to 1866. Myra was an ardent Southern supporter and dedicated Christian, probably in the same mold as Eliza Fain. In her diary, Myra makes mention of "cousin Sam Inman," age twenty-three, who came from Texas, possibly around 1860–1861, to "get [his] inheritance from his mother's estate"; he ended up joining the Confederate army. Sadly, Miss Inman also makes mention of Samuel's death from typhoid-pneumonia in a diary entry on February 19, 1862, with Sam's demise taking place the previous February 7 in Sneedville, Hancock County, exactly two months after the Byrd raid. Just as important, the same entry noted Sam as being "captain of his company and an excellent young man."[98] Beyond this information, and like the jail records, nothing is recorded by Miss Inman regarding Samuel's unit name, service dates, actions participated in, etc. Furthermore, a review of Civil War records for Tennessee revealed several possibilities for Samuel but nothing conclusive. So, in summary, if Captain Samuel Inman was in charge of a Rebel company, was it operating in the Hancock and northern Hawkins area less than two months before his death? If so, Sam Inman could very well be our man—the "Serg't Inman" noted as the "arresting officer" in so many Knoxville jail records during December 1861. But until further information is forthcoming, it's admitted the identity of "Serg't Inman" remains muddled.

After the Greens, the next man arrested was a William L. Richardson, age eighteen of Hancock County, who was seized on Monday, December 9. A review of census records failed to locate an exact match in Hancock County, but this man may be either William Richie, age eighteen, a farmhand for Isaac Parkey's family, which lived in the Alanthus Hill area of Four Mile District of Hancock,[99] or Willie Richards, age eighteen, who lived in Mill Bend, District Four of Hawkins County, with the Wm. Thomas family.[100] Like the first two men, jail records noted Richardson was arrested by "Serg't Inman" and accused of membership in Byrd's company.

On the following day, Tuesday, December 10, Confederate authorities arrested several more Loyalists in an apparent sweep through Lee Valley, an area located on the north side of Clinch Mountain in Hawkins County. Those arrested included Jesse D. Berry, age forty-one; James L. Berry, age twenty-one; W.D. Cobb, age forty-five; Edward S. McGinnis; and John Wolf, age fifty-two. All five, with possible exception of Wolf, lived in Lee Valley in close proximity to Captain Byrd and other Loyalists. The Berrys, according to a census, were farmers by trade, with James the apparent young son of Jesse D., living next door to his father. Like the others, authorities accused the Berrys of membership in Byrd's company, with young James additionally charged with shooting and wounding a man in Captain John W. Phillips's E Company during the fight. The third man, W.D. Cobb is believed to be Winstered Cobb, another Loyalist arrested by "Serg't Inman," who also lived in Lee Valley and faced accusations of consorting with Byrd's company.

The other two apprehensions that day included Edward S. McGinnis and a John Wolf. Edward is identified in a census as E.S. McGinnis, age twenty-four, a school teacher who, like the Berrys and Cobb, was a resident of Lee Valley, Hawkins County. The previous September, Confederate authorities had arrested McGinnis on treason charges, which culminated in an appearance before the East Tennessee Confederate District Court in Knoxville, where he received a light sentence by taking the oath of allegiance. Arrested this time around by "Serg't Inman," McGinnis faced charges of being "found with a union company." While the company name failed to be noted, it's presumed to have been Byrd's. Also, McGinnis's individual jail record appears to have incorrectly noted his residence as Hancock instead of Hawkins.

The fifth man arrested by "Serg't Inman" that day, a John Wolf, lived in Hawkins County and, like young Joseph Green, faced accusations of shooting and wounding a member of Captain Phillips's E Company. Unfortunately, insufficient or conflicting information regarding John Wolf prevented a positive identification. But if John's "Hawkins County residence" is correct, as noted in his jail entry, there may be only one possible John Wolf in the 1860 census for Hawkins County—a J.L. Wolf, age sixty, who lived and farmed in the Mooresburg area.[101] On the other hand, several John Wolfs are listed in the Hancock County 1860 census, but marked differences in ages precluded several, except for two. The first and maybe best candidate is John Wolf, age sixty, who lived and farmed in the War Creek area of the Walker District of Hancock, followed by John Wolf, age fifty-eight, who lived and farmed at Yellow Spring in the Sumpter District of Hancock. Interestingly, John Wolf at War Creek lived only a short distance from several known secessionists who later were indicted for involvement in the Byrd raid.[102]

As Confederates continued the December wave of arrests following the clash with Byrd's company, "Serg't Inman" took Ambrose Hopkins, age thirty-four, of Hawkins County into custody on Wednesday, December 11, 1861, and—like the others—charged him with being part of Byrd's company. But similar to John Wolf, the identification of Hopkins could not be fully confirmed using 1860 census records for either Hawkins or Hancock Counties. Although one possibility found in the census for Ambrose Hopkins may be Abram Hopkins, age twenty-four, son of Jabez Hopkins, who lived in the Sneedville area or District Six of Hancock County, this man admittedly represents a wild card. The Knoxville jail record for Ambrose Hopkins stated his age as thirty-four and a resident of Hawkins County.[103] Granted, Ambrose may have only recently moved into the area after the 1860 census or lived elsewhere, thus explaining his apparent absence from the local census.

On Thursday, December 12, 1861, authorities arrested Ephraim Byrd, age twenty-nine, son of Captain Byrd. Ephraim's jail record fails to mention the arresting officer, although "Serg't Inman" is suspected of having made this arrest as well. Of course Ephraim, or Enoch Byrd, as listed in the 1860 Hancock census, lived in the Holland District of Hancock.

Two days later, on Saturday, December 14, Inman makes yet another arrest, an N. Hurley, a thirty-nine-year-old Hawkins County man accused of membership in Byrd's company and of being a "deserter from Gen Rozencrant." If the latter accusation is a reference to Union general William Rosecrans, it would seem a bit odd noting it under the apparent circumstances. Also, despite an age and county difference between jail and census records, N. Hurley is believed to be Nehemiah Harley, age seventy-five, a resident of Sneedville, District Six of Hancock. It's also possible that Nehemiah is a brother to another arrestee, an M. Hurley, or according to the census, Moses Hurley, age sixty-eight, who lived in the same area. But doubt remains concerning the accuracy of Nehemiah's identification and Moses's as well, due in part that neither man hailed from the War Creek or Lee Valley areas where Unionists seemed concentrated.

After Hurley's arrest, the ongoing activity to suppress and arrest local Loyalists in the area appeared to drop off, this pause reflecting a possible temporary change of focus or priorities by Confederate authorities. But on Christmas Day 1861, with lightening speed, the arrests in the Hancock-Hawkins area quickly resumed with several taking place, according to jail records. On that day, the following seven were taken into custody: Thos. Johnson and Martin Murrell of Hawkins; John Waddles, G.M. Dougherty and Wm. Berbee, all Hancock residents; along with Stephen Frost and Jacob Myers, both from Lee County, Virginia. Unfortunately the identification of Thos. or Thomas Johnson is somewhat muddled by the sheer fact of there being at least five Thomas Johnsons in the 1860 census living in and around Hancock and Hawkins Counties. Even so, it's felt that Thos. Johnson, age twenty-nine, might well be the Thomas Johnson identified in the census living in Lee Valley, Hawkins County, a few doors from fellow Unionist Wintered Cobb (W.D. Cobb), and likewise the same Thomas Johnson as noted in the court and jail records, with the latter record accusing him of being a member of Byrd's company.

Martin Murrill, another Christmas Day arrestee, is identified in the census as Martin Murrel, age nineteen, a Lee Valley, Hawkins County resident and farm laborer who lived in the household of Rebecca Berton (Burton?).[104] Interestingly, Rebecca resided next door to Unionist Winstered Cobb, already identified in jail records as W.D. Cobb. In addition, Martin's jail record spelled his last name as Murrell and incorrectly gave his residence as Hancock. The jail record for Martin goes on to accuse him of membership in Byrd's company. The next man, John Waddles of Hancock County is identified in the census as John Waddle, age nineteen, a resident of War Creek or Holland District of Hancock and a close neighbor to the Byrd family. Arrested by "Serg't Inman," authorities accused John of being a member of Byrd's company.

The jail record for Jacob Myers listed his arrest by "Serg't Inman" and residency the same as Ephraim Byrd and Stephen Frost—Lee County,

Virginia. Myers, like the others, was accused of membership in Captain Byrd's company, but more significantly, the jail record further accused Myers of being a bridge burner. Interestingly, other historical sources seem to confirm this bridge-burning accusation by indicating Jacob, along with Daniel Smith, as later being "tried and found guilty of having some connection" in burning the Lick Creek bridge in Greene County, about fifteen miles from Greeneville, Tennessee.[105] Those convictions would result in Confederate authorities sending both men to prison at Tuscaloosa, Alabama.

Stephen Frost of Lee County, Virginia, is identified in the census as Stephen Frost age thirty, a distiller, formerly of War Creek in Hancock's Holland District. Stephen Frost, like his former neighbor and fellow Unionist, Ephraim Byrd, apparently relocated his family to Lee County some time around the start of the war, probably for protection and to escape Rebel harassment in the Hancock area. But while still a resident of Hancock, Frost lived in close proximity to the Unionist Green and Byrd families. Frost was arrested by "Serg't Inman" and faced charges of "assisting [Jacob] Myers to escape." Another arrestee, G.M. Dougherty, is identified in the census as George M. Daughtry, age twenty-six, a brick mason who lived in the Sneedville area of District Six of Hancock County.[106] Daugherty was arrested by "Serg't Inman," and like his fellow compatriots, he was accused of being connected or consorting with Byrd's company.

The last of the seven Christmas Day arrestees, Wm. Berbee of Hancock, may in fact be William Buttery, age twenty-six, a farm laborer who lived in the War Creek area of the Holland District of Hancock.[107] Buttery's identification is plausible since he lived only a few doors from the Unionist Green and Byrd families. Berbee, or Buttery, arrested by "Serg't Inman," was said to have been yet another member of Byrd's company. But two other possible identifications for Berbee are William Berry, age eighteen, son of Lewis Berry, who lived in the Alanthus Hill area of Four Mile District of Hancock, or William Berry, age thirteen, of Lee Valley, Hawkins County, the young son of J.D. or Jesse D. Berry. Of course, as noted already, Jesse D. Berry the elder had been arrested about two weeks before and accused of involvement with Byrd's company.

In addition to those above and according to Knoxville jail records, Confederate authorities arrested several other Hawkins and Hancock Unionists during this period, but for unexplained reasons, they either had no comments or only sketchy details in their respective jail records. They included the following men: Wm. Jones; A.T. Brooks; Jno. Wyatt, age fifty-two; George Trewiit, believed to be George Trent, age twenty; and M.

Hurley, believed to be Moses Hurley, all of Hancock. Those arrested from Hawkins County were Jno. Good, age seventeen; Jno. Wright, age forty-nine; Emmerson Walker; Marion Walker; and Harry Walker.

Wm. Jones is believed to be William B. Jones, age eighteen, found in the census and who lived with the John Bloomer family in the War Creek area of the Walker District of Hancock.[108] Jones's jail record contained no comments. Two other possibilities for Jones found in the census are William Johns, age twenty-one, a farmer and apparent son of Rial Johns, who lived in the same area as William B. Jones, or maybe William H. Jonas, age thirty-five, a physician who lived in the town of Sneedville.

A.T. Brooks, another man arrested from Hancock, according to census may be Alfred Brooks, age sixteen, son of Thomas Brooks, who lived in the Sneedville area of the Davis District of Hancock. Other than Brooks's name, county name and age, his jail record contained no comments. Jno. Wyatt, age fifty-two, is identified in census as John Wiat, a distiller who lived in the Sneedville area of the Davis District of Hancock.[109] Wyatt's immediate next-door neighbor was Unionist militia captain Joel Jarvis. Like Brooks, other than name, county name and age, Wyatt's jail record is void of any comments. George Trewitt is believed to be George W. Trent, age twenty, who lived in the War Creek area or Holland District of Hancock. Trewitt's, or Trent's, neighbors included the Green and Byrd families.[110]

As noted previously, M. Hurley is identified in the census as Moses Hurley, age sixty-eight, a day laborer and resident of the Sneedville area in District Six, Hancock. As mentioned, Moses may be a relative or even brother to N. Hurley, believed to be Nehemiah Hurley, who authorities apparently arrested on December 14. An arrest date for Moses is missing, but it's thought it took place the same day as Nehemiah's. As far as those from Hawkins, such as Jno Good, age seventeen, a census record wasn't located or couldn't be reliably related or verified. But one possibility for Good is John Gowings, age thirteen, the mulatto son of Riada Gowings, who lived in the War Gap area of District Three of Hawkins. Coincidently, the Gowings family lived right next door to Captain John W. Phillips of Company E, Forty-third Infantry, CSA. Yet still another remote possibility for Good is John A. Guins, age eighteen, who lived with the Thomas Guins family in the Sneedville area of District Six, Hancock. Other than county name and age, there were no comments in Good's jail record. Lastly, there is Jno. Wright, age forty-nine, of Hawkins, who may be John Wright, age thirty-five, found in the census and who was a shoemaker that lived in Lee Valley[111] or possibly John

Wright, age fifty, who lived with the William Wright family in District Thirteen of Hawkins.[112] Other than county origin and age, no comments existed in Wright's jail record.

The three Walker men were identified based on 1860 census records as Horry (Harry?), age twenty-one, Marion, age twenty-three, and Emberson (Emerson?) Walker, age seventeen, the sons of James and Elizabeth Walker, who resided in District Fourteen of Hawkins County.[113] William G. Brownlow made reference to two of the brothers in a diary he kept while imprisoned at Castle Fox in December 1861. According to Parson, authorities had arrested the Walkers for "talking union talk," but their respective jail records also accused them of "aiding Lincoln's army."

The arrests carried out by Confederates after the Byrd raid in December 1861 ultimately netted about thirty-five Lincolnite prisoners in the Hancock-Hawkins area. As the records reflected, Confederates took many of those arrested under armed guard to Knoxville and tried them for treason before the East Tennessee Confederate District Court in January 1862. But most historical accounts during this turbulent period suggest much higher numbers of arrests and related deaths of Union people, not only in Hancock and Hawkins Counties, but all over east Tennessee—at least far more than documented in the Knoxville jail records. With fear and panic obviously rampant since the bridge burnings and subsequent actions by both sides further intensifying and escalating already angry feelings, the jail journal numbers no doubt fell far short, only representing the tip of the iceberg.

CHAPTER 7

Castle Fox Prison,
Then the Trials

As the Rebel reign of terror spread through the hills and valleys of
east Tennessee during November and December 1861, the town
of Knoxville continued filling with Unionist political prisoners. During
this period, it's estimated that Confederates arrested a thousand or more
citizens suspected of Union or Loyalist involvement, shipping them off
quickly to Knoxville to await trial before the Confederate district court.
To accommodate such large numbers, authorities established a temporary
prison on the corner of Main and Prince Streets to handle overflow from
the infamous county or Knoxville jail. Even the Bell House Hotel, one of the
more prominent establishments in Knoxville at this time, housed a number
of Unionist prisoners. Despite these measures, it's known for various reasons
that many never saw the inside of a courtroom or their due day in court,
including some of the Hancock and Hawkins men arrested that December.

The charges against Unionist prisoners varied greatly. Authorities
ultimately found only a handful of prisoners having actual participation
in the bridge burnings and a somewhat larger number possessing prior
knowledge of the plot. Still others like the men from Hancock and Hawkins
Counties were imprisoned for taking up arms and being part of Unionist
home guards. But many more, possibly a majority, may have endured arrest
"simply because of known Unionist sympathies." One local Confederate
officer readily suspected that "old political animosities and private grudges"
formed the basis for many of the arrests and concluded "bad men among
our friends" had taken opportunity to hunt down "all those against whom

William G. "Parson" Brownlow's health never fully recovered from the stark conditions, poor diet and physical abuse endured while imprisoned. *Courtesy of Tennessee State Library and Archives.*

they entertain any feeling of dislike." Not long after this period, the Confederate War Department admitted as much when stating, "It's not only possible but probable that in the confusion and disorder of the times some innocent men have been confounded with the guilty."[114]

During the "reign of the rebels" in early December, authorities arrested William G. "Parson" Brownlow and imprisoned him at Castle Fox for nearly a month. Parson, a renowned Union man, editor of the *Knoxville Whig* newspaper and later governor of Tennessee, kept a diary during his imprisonment. It gave a glimpse of the daily events, jail conditions and other work carried on by Confederate authorities during his imprisonment. Jailed on the evening of December 6, 1861, Brownlow soon after chronicled in his diary the horrible jail conditions and harsh treatment, both physical and psychological, experienced by the mostly Unionist jail population.[115] The following are exerts from Brownlow's writings:

But I was thrown into this jail…where I found about 150 Union men, old and young, representing all professions. The jail was so crowded that on the lower floor we had not room for all to lie down at one time. The prisoners took rest by turns, a portion standing while the others slept. There was not a chair, bench, stool, block, table, or any other article of furniture, in the building, save a dirty wooden bucket and a tin cup, used for watering the occupants of the room. A bucketful would not go round, as the weather was at times warm and many of the prisoners were feverish. To supply them with water, a hogshead [barrel] was placed by the side of the jail, and a boy with a cart hauled water through the day. One prisoner at a time was allowed to go out with the bucket and draw it full, under an escort of bayonets. About 24 men were kept around the jail in arms, and on the inside at the windows, which were allowed to be up in daylight only to give us fresh air. Through the windows we could see these dirty, sweating, insulting, and abusive Rebel soldiers go to the hogshead and wash their hands and faces in it. I remonstrated, telling these ill-bred fellows that this water was our only dependence for drinking- water. The reply was, "By G———d, sir, we will have you know that where a Jeff Davis man washes his face and hands is good enough for any d———d Lincolnite to drink!" We of course had no remedy to submit.

Despite these conditions, Brownlow admitted while in jail to being allowed to have his meals delivered from home, three times a day, which in many cases he claimed sharing with older prisoners, some of whom were sick and infirmed. As such, it is safe to say that few, if any, of the other prisoners were afforded this same privilege. Brownlow went on to further describe the prison food, likely the same as eaten by the men from Hancock-Hawkins counties:

The food given the prisoners to eat was not fit for a good and trusty dog to devour. It was composed of scraps and leavings of a dirty hotel kept by the jailer and deputy marshal of the Confederacy—the meat and bread sometimes half raw, sometimes burned, and always a scanty supply.

As this vile treatment and loathsome food produced disease, and, added to colds, often fell upon the bowels, the Rebel brutes who guarded us were furnished with additional opportunities for offering us personal indignity.

Expanding further on the psychological treatment, Brownlow noted,

We were all cursed and denounced both day and night. In marching us out and into the prison, we were ordered to "walk faster," and threaten with the bayonet if we did not obey…The feeling (by Confederates) was, as a general thing, that any sort of treatment and fare were "too good for a set of d———d Union-shriekers and bridge-burners," as they styled all the prisoners.

Included from Brownlow's diary are other important entries that may relate to the confrontation that took place on December 7, with Byrd's militia and other Lincolnists.[116] They follow:

> *Wed., Dec. 11*
> *Fifteen prisoners came in today from Greene and Hancock counties, charged with having been armed as Union men and accustomed to drill.*
>
> *Friday, Dec. 13*
> *Three more prisoners in today from Hancock and Hawkins Counties. Charged as usual—Union men, attached to a company of Home Guards.*
>
> *Saturday, Dec. 14*
> *Three more prisoners from the upper counties were brought in today. They speak of the outrages perpetrated by these rebel troops, and of their murderous spirit.*
>
> *Tuesday, Dec. 17*
> *Tonight two brothers named Walker, came in from Hawkins County charged with having "talked Union talk."*

The entries for December 11, 13 and 14 no doubt relate to the confrontation with Byrd's militia on December 7. In fact, the timing alone of these entries and the raid on Byrd suggest a possible link, especially when considering the proximity of Hancock-Hawkins Counties and Mooresburg to Knoxville. Also during this period, Confederates utilized Knoxville as a primary jail and processing point for Unionist prisoners arrested in east Tennessee.

Also supporting Brownlow's accounts and other cascading events after December 7 are court minutes from the East Tennessee Confederate District Court at Knoxville for the months of November 1861 through January 1862, which document court appearances and trials of many of the prisoners from Hawkins and Hancock Counties. In addition to court minutes, the Knoxville jail journal referenced earlier contains considerable information on civilians or Lincolnites arrested during this time, not only for bridge burning but for being "up in arms" and assorted other crimes against the Confederacy. Along with individual names, each jail record in many instances includes each man's age, county residence, charge or charges pending, arresting officer's name and the prisoner's disposition.

The East Tennessee Confederate District Court prepared to convene in Knoxville on November 25, 1861, as the Knoxville jail and other holding areas continued filling with east Tennessee Unionists and other political prisoners arrested after the bridge burnings. The court had critical business and cases needing adjudication that fall and winter, with none probably more important than the pending trials for scores of political prisoners. Although this court session would last until the end of January 1862, the court was severely hampered the first few weeks in conducting business, due to the unexplained absence of Judge West Humphreys until January. Strangely, court records offered no explanations or hints regarding Humphreys's absence or whereabouts. Consequently, Loyalist prisoners, including those from Hawkins and Hancock Counties, were forced to linger in the local jails, no doubt under horrible conditions for up to six weeks longer than necessary, waiting for their day in court.

On Wednesday, December 18, 1861, during the judge's absence, the first group of men from Hancock-Hawkins Counties were brought into court in custody of the marshal and District Attorney John Crozier Ramsey. This group, mixed in with about fifty prisoners making appearances that day, included A.T. Brooks, Wm. L. Richardson, George Trewitt (Trent), John Wyatt and Jackson Bird, all of Hancock, along with John Wright and the three Walker brothers, Emerson, Marion and Harry, all from Hawkins. Interestingly, two of the Walker brothers had just been jailed the evening before, according to Brownlow's diary. After a brief appearance before the court, each man agreed to a $1,000 bond in order to guarantee their presence at the January session "to answer charges as may be preferred against them."[117] Most of these men had no comments in their respective jail records, and the court records lacked specifics or any mention of serious charges. As such, the court apparently took what amounted to a recognizance bond from each prisoner, with authorities probably concluding the charges against them were either minor or less threatening in nature. Also, while the court didn't specifically state this, the men in this group may have been released, with their only requirement being a return appearance before the court in January.

On January 13, 1862, the East Tennessee Confederate District Court reconvened, this time with Judge West Humphreys presiding.[118] The first case of the day involved Stokely D. Trent, age thirty-five, who lived in War Creek of Hancock County. Trent was brought before the court with another man, James Moore. District Attorney Ramsey stated that he had "no written charges against either man" and dismissed the case. Both men took the required oath of allegiance to the Confederate States, paid court costs and were allowed to leave. Interestingly, Stokely not only gained his freedom that day but survived the war and later served on the grand jury in Hawkins County, which brought a murder indictment against many of the Confederates accused in the Byrd raid.

Later that morning, A.T Brooks of Hancock and John Wright of Hawkins appeared with several other men, fulfilling promises to return before the court, as was conditional for their release in December. District Attorney Ramsey entered a *nolle prosequi*, effectively abandoning his suit against both. The men, in effect, "confessed judgment," took the oath of allegiance and paid their respective court cost. Later that same day, the three Walker brothers from Hawkins County made their own appearances, but probably to their personal relief and amazement, the court rendered "there were no charges preferred against them" and dismissed the case. The Walkers took the oath, paid court costs and no doubt left soon after. Near the end of that same day, Jackson Bird of Hancock made his return appearance to court in the presence of District Attorney Ramsey. Like the Walkers, the court concluded there were "no written charges preferred against" Bird, so after repeating the oath and paying his security, Jackson was set free. Interestingly, the court record noted that Wilson Willis acted as Byrd's security in the cause. Willis appears to be Will Willis, a thirty-eight-year-old Lee Valley farmer who lived a few doors from Jackson's two brothers, James A. and Lias (Levi) Bird and their father, Captain William K. Byrd.

After Bird's appearance, eleven days transpired before another Hancock-Hawkins man appeared in court, which occurred Friday, January 24, 1862, the last official day of the court's term.[119] The first case of the day involved Joseph Green, or Josephus Green, as noted in the Knoxville jail record, who was led alone into the court room. Green was identified in the census as the sixteen-year-old son of James Green, age forty, living in the War Creek area of the Holland District, Hancock County. Both James and Joseph lived only two doors from Alfred Green, age thirty-three, a possible relative and maybe the same Alfred Green, according to court records, who acted as Joseph's security. The court considered Joseph's "youthfulness" and released him upon entering into a "conditional security" of $200, to be voided based on his future good behavior. Of course, Joseph or Josephus, along with Wm. L. Green, another War Creek resident, had been arrested December 8, 1861, and charged with "going to Kentucky for arms and men." Both William and Joseph received discharges on January 24, 1862, after taking the oath of allegiance to the Confederate States and entering into the security bond noted above.

Later that Friday, Stephen Frost, more recently a resident of Lee County, Virginia, but formerly of War Creek area in the Holland District of Hancock, made his appearance in court. While a resident of War Creek, Frost lived only a few doors from the Greens. In regard to the cause against Frost, age thirty-one, the court record, like most other defendants, lacked sufficient detail but concluded the case against Frost as a matter of "general civil jurisdiction," maybe in part due to the fact Frost claimed residency in Lee County Virginia, rather than Hancock County or Tennessee. Frost's court appearance ended with him "acknowledging himself indebted" to the Confederate States, exhibiting a wiliness to "conform to the laws of the said Confederate States" and entering into a bond of $1,000. According to jail records, authorities had arrested Frost on December 25, 1861 and had charged him with "assisting Jacob Myers to escape." Of course, Myers, arrested the same day, would be convicted of involvement in the Lick Creek Bridge burning. More important, it would be Myers, not Frost, ushered off to the Tuscaloosa prison on January 26, 1862. Next to be led into the courtroom behind Frost was Geo., or George, M. Daugherty of the Sneedville area of Hancock County. Like the action against Stephen Frost, the court found the case against Daugherty a matter of "general civil jurisdiction." Afterward, Daugherty agreed to a $1,000 bond.

While Jackson Byrd, the Walker brothers, Joseph Green, Stephen Frost and George M. Daugherty apparently gained their freedom, the same relief would remain out of reach for another Byrd family member and several others from Hancock and Hawkins Counties. Immediately after discharging Daugherty, Ephraim Byrd was brought into court along with ten other men in custody of the marshal before Judge Humphreys. Besides Ephraim, it appears at least six in this group were residents of Hawkins-Hancock area.[120] Also by now, most of these men, according to jail records, had spent close to six weeks in the horrendous confines of the Knoxville prison. Along with Ephraim, they included W.B. Thomson, John Waddel, Edward S. McGinnis, W.D. Cobb, W.L. Richardson, N. Hurley, Thomas Johnson, Martin Murril, John Headerick and James T. Berry.

With this group of men, District Attorney John Crozier Ramsey brought his most serious charge to date against any Hawkins or Hancock prisoner— the crime of treason under a writ of habeas corpus. The specific charges against the men, while not fully detailed in the court record, stated "the cause being fully heard and it appearing also to the satisfaction of the court that there is sufficient evidence to hold them…for treason."

Afterward, Ramsey made a motion to the court—and it was accepted—that Ephraim and the others be turned over to local military authorities and held as prisoners of war. Although the court record failed to elaborate, Knoxville jail records indicate Ephraim and twenty other men being sent, probably via rail two days later on Sunday, January 26, 1862, to the Confederate prison at Tuscaloosa, Alabama, for an undetermined period. (For more information on the men sent to the Tuscaloosa prison on January 26, 1862, see Appendix B.)

After leading Ephraim Byrd and the others away under armed guard, destined for prison, another Hancock County man—a John Wilborn—was immediately escorted into the courtroom with several other men.[121] Wilborn is identified, according to the 1860 census, as John Willbourn, age nineteen, son of Lewis Willbourn, who lived in the Sneedville area of the Davis District of Hancock County.[122] John's jail record noted him as a member of Byrd's company. The Willbourn family lived only two doors from Unionist militia leader Joel Jarvis and John Wiat, with Wiat already identified as Jno Wyatt, age fifty-two. Young John Willbourn held some distinction for being the only man in Byrd's company known to have been arrested ahead of the raid, three days prior on Wednesday, December 4, 1861. Besides John, the other six men who made appearances included James Clark, David Moore, Jesse Price, D.H. Bone, Moses Price and W.M. Bone, with none of the six having any apparent connection with Hancock or Hawkins Counties. But fortunately for all seven including Willbourn, the court ruled that there was "not sufficient evidence to hold" them for treason. With that decision, John and the others took the oath prior to being released.

Interestingly, and according to Jesse Price's jail record, four of the men released with Willbourn were arrested at the same time while "making their way to Lincoln's camp at Wyoming, VA."[123] With Jesse, they included Moses Price, son of Jesse; Wm. H. Bone; and D.H. Bone. Jesse's jail record noted that the four tried to escape when first approached by Confederates, initiating the arrest. The two Prices hailed from Ash City, North Carolina, while the Bones' residences and ages went unrecorded. Neither of the Bones could be located in the 1860 Tennessee census.

The winter session of the East Tennessee Confederate District Court ended on Friday, January 24, 1862. With the court's closing, it appears that as many as 10 of the 35 men arrested from Hancock and Hawkins County following the raid on Byrd failed to receive their day in court during this concluding session. On the other hand, if in fact they did, their respective court records are either missing or went unrecorded. This group included: Jesse D. Berry,

James Buttre (Buttery), Jno Good, Ambrose Hopkins, Jno Wolf, all of Hawkins County; and Wm BerBee, Wm. L. Green, M. Hurly, Wm. Jones and Jno Livison (Levicy), all of Hancock County. But in reviewing the jail records for these men, three of the ten appeared to have been released due to suspected lack of evidence, etc. They included Jesse D. Berry, whose jail record noted him freed after taking the oath on January 13, 1862, as was the case for Wm. L. Green, released the following day on January 14, and Ambrose Hopkins, also noted as being released on January 14 but without mention of any oath being taken. For Jno Good, Wm. Berbee and Wm Jones, their respective jail records lacked "final dispositions," but it's believed they were released as well. Nevertheless, it must be noted that several of these same Hawkins-Hancock men released by the court during January were apparently rearrested later in 1862, with several ending up on a Confederate list of prisoners at Macon, Georgia, in July 1862.[124] That prisoner list and associated letter was addressed to Colonel (W.M.) Churchwell, Confederate provost marshal for east Tennessee, from Colonel L.H. Carter of Headquarters Tenth Battalion, Georgia Volunteers, CSA, guard of prisoners, who listed 110 or so political prisoners being held at Macon.

As far as the others in this group of ten, neither James Buttre (Buttery) nor Jno Livison (Levicy) had individual jail records, but they were part of a separate jailhouse notation, indicating that both were "sent to Tuscaloosa on Dec. 12, 1861," less than a week after the Byrd raid. As far as Jno Wolf, his jail record stated that he was "discharged on application of Col. Rains," with no date or other details specified. M. Hurly's jail record noted him being "sent to Tuscaloosa," with no date given.[125] Unfortunately, with the Hurlys or Hurleys, like a few others, some doubt remains as to who exactly and how many persons authorities actually sent to Tuscaloosa on January 26.

The absence of the these men from court records shouldn't be surprising and can be attributed to several things, not the least of which was simple human error or more likely the sheer confusion and pandemonium that reigned after the bridge burnings and the continued Unionist uprising following those treasonous acts. Also, the court records in some cases are fragmented with unexplained gaps, while the Knoxville jail records have further inconsistencies, which quickly become apparent when trying to match arrestees with court records. Of course, for many Loyalists jailed during this violent period, especially in the country or remote areas of east Tennessee, court hearings were few and seldom offered as an option to Unionists. Many times, Loyalists and their families were threatened with harm, imprisoned without hearings or, at worst, sometimes shot or killed because of their political beliefs. Of course, in some situations, so-called accusations against Unionists resulted from longstanding personal grudges or bias rather than any overt or treasonous activities by the individual.

Before continuing further, it must be noted that, in reviewing the census, court and Knoxville jail records for this chapter, misleading information was uncovered concerning Jackson Bird. On the court record side, and as depicted, Jackson was set free on January 13, 1862, but Knoxville jail record notations (separate from individual records) seem to reflect an entirely different disposition for Bird. To begin with, one jail notation has Jackson Bird, along with Jno Livison, Stokely Trent, and James Buttre being sent to Tuscaloosa on December 12, 1861. On the other hand, Stokely Trent's court record, like Bird's, stated both men were tried and released the same January day.[126]

Of course, James Buttre is believed to be James Buttery, age forty-one, of Lee Valley, Hawkins County, and the same James Buttery noted previously as failing to receive a court appearance in January 1861 after his apparent arrest the previous month. Interestingly, James Buttery of Lee Valley resided next door to Levi Bird (Lias Bird in census) and Captain Byrd and a short distance from James A. Bird.[127] It also appears that authorities had arrested James Buttery's son, David, back in September, only to release him after taking the oath.

The other man, Jno Livison, is believed to be one of two John Levicys found in census living in the War Gap area in the Levicy District of Hancock County, John G. Levicy, age twenty, or John Levicy, age seventeen, son of George Levicy.[128] Both of these men were neighbors and, as such, likely relatives. Just as interesting, a J. Levisy of Hancock County was found to be included in Colonel Carter's list of prisoners held at Macon, Georgia, in July 1862—more evidence that a Levisy was, in fact, sent to prison at Tuscaloosa on December 12 or possibly rearrested later after the January trials and then sent to prison.

The second jailhouse notation containing a J. Bird and others is titled "ordered to Tuscaloosa by Court martial."[129] While lacking a date, it contained the following names and explanations:

> *J. Cate*—*in arms against C.S.*
> *M. Cate*—[Same]
> *L. Cate*—[Same]
> *C.C. Howard*—*prisoner of war*
> *Garrett Hall*—[Same]
> *J.H. Hickman*—*in arms against the C.S.*

H. Langston—[Same]
W.V. Thompson—[Same]
Joel Hogan of Cliff's Co.—*in arms against the C. S.*
J. Bird—*Rebellion*

Of course, it's possible and readily admitted, some or all of the above references are due to there being more than one individual arrested by the same name, including that of Jackson Bird. But the timing of these records, both court and jail, occurring so soon after the Byrd raid and in conjunction with other men arrested and clearly identified as Hancock and Hawkins men is justification for believing that some, if not all, of the jailhouse information does in fact relate to Jackson Bird, son of Captain Byrd of Hancock County. Furthermore, all of those included in the above undated list of ten "ordered to Tuscaloosa by Court martial" appear to be included on the Tuscaloosa list for January 26, except for Hickman, Langston and, of course, J. Bird. Also relevant is the fact that individual jailhouse records for Hickman and Langston, while lacking dates, do appear to support this second notation of being "sent to Tuscaloosa." Also noteworthy is that Colonel Carter's list of Unionist prisoners held at Macon, Georgia, in July 1862 appears to include both a Hickman and Langston H., while noting their residence as Sevier County, which corresponds with their jail records. In reviewing 1860 census records, J.H. Hickman in the jail notation is believed to be Jas or James Hickman, age thirty-four, a resident of Strawberry Plains, District Twelve of Sevier County.[130] Jas or James lived close to several Cates, in fact, just four to five doors away from J.H. Cate, an apparent fellow prisoner. Authorities accused James in the court-martial of being "found in arms." The other man, H. Langston, also found in the census, is believed to be Sevier County farmer Harvey Langston, age twenty-three, living in the Henry Roads area of District Eight.[131] Harvey, like James, was accused of being "found in arms" against the Confederate States and, along with Hickman, apparently sent to Tuscaloosa.

A third piece of evidence, which supports the prospect that Jackson Bird of Hancock County was sent to Tuscaloosa, is a reference noted previously in Colonel L.H. Carter's letter regarding east Tennessee political prisoners being held in Macon. In that letter, a J. Bird of Scott County, rather than of Hancock County, was noted as a Macon prisoner. This group of prisoners, destined for exchange, was en route from Tuscaloosa to Atlanta as part of a return trip to east Tennessee, only to be held up temporarily by Confederate authorities at Macon.

In summary, it's felt the court record depicting Jackson Bird being released on January 13, 1862, does reflect Jackson Byrd of Hancock County, son of Captain William K. Byrd. On the other hand, until additional information is obtained, the J., or possibly Jackson, Bird sent to Tuscaloosa is thought to be another Bird/Byrd from Sevier or Scott County, rather than Hancock. That conclusion is based partly on the information from Colonel Carter's list of prisoners held at Macon and other 1860 census data.

Along with the Knoxville jailhouse notations mentioned above, there were other notations separate of the individual records, which contained additional references to Hancock-Hawkins county men. One such notation contained a "list of prisoners in the Knoxville jail on March 15, 1862," which noted the following two Hawkins-Hancock men. The first is a Rich'd Robinson, age thirty-two, of Hawkins, who was charged with horse stealing and for claiming he was "pressed" to commit the act "by order of his officer." Rich is believed to be Richard Robinson, found in the census as a farm laborer who lived in the Mooresburg area of District Twelve.[132] The second man was Jno McGehee, age twenty-five, Hancock, charged with "desertion" and identified in the census as John McGhee, who appears to be the same man arrested and brought before the court back on September 12, 1861, and then released with several other Hancock-Hawkins men after taking the oath. This latest charge of desertion probably resulted from John joining or being forced to join a Confederate unit against his wishes, only later to desert and be rearrested.[133]

Still another jail notation indicated prisoners "committed [to Knoxville jail?] March 21, 1862" after being "captured by Capt. H.K. Legg's company." Captain Legg appears to be Captain Henry K. Legg, Company D, Fifth (McClellan's) Tennessee Cavalry Battalion, CSA, a unit formed in August 1861 from the Hancock-Hawkins area.[134] This list noted one prisoner from Hawkins County, an H. Watkins, but Watkins failed to be located in the 1860 census as living in either Hancock or Hawkins County. Still further, another jailhouse record noted "prisoners committed March 30, 1862," listing a "Wm. Goins age 19, of Hawkins County." Goins had been charged with "recruiting for Lincoln and [being a] Fry recruit." The latter comment is a possible reference to membership in Captain David Fry's Company F, Second Tennessee Infantry, USA. Along with Goins and Captain Fry, this same "committal list" included several other men from Greene County, who were all facing the same charges as Goins. Lastly, while not ignoring completely the Hawkins County residency noted by Colonel Carter for Goins, another possible identification for this man may be a Wm. Goens, age eighteen, listed in the census as a farm laborer living with the Samuel Seal family at War Creek in the Murrel District of Hancock County.[135]

In summary, of the men from the Hawkins-Hancock area sent to Tuscaloosa, most did in fact survive the Tuscaloosa portion of their imprisonment, at least according to Colonel Carter's list of prisoners at Macon in July 1862.[136] That list and the associated letter written by Colonel L.H. Carter divided the men into two groups. The following is the text of Colonel Carter's letter and a list of the men believed from Hawkins-Hancock area, under respective group headings of "having took the oath" or "willing to take the oath."

> *I sent a list of the Political Prisoners from E. Tenn. to Gen. E.K. Smith a few days ago. I now transmit the same to you calling your special attention to their cases knowing as I do that the Confederate government does not pursue a policy that consigns men to imprisonment without a fair trial and never refuses protection to those who have taken the oath of allegiance and stand un-condemned of having committed any crime. I will feel myself under obligation to you if you will look into their cases. Release them if all right or let me have the facts as to their guilt. For it is quite unpleasant to hear prisoners in my charge who claim to have had no trial and profess themselves willing to do all required of citizens known to have been disloyal. The taking of the oath of allegiance is all the proclamation published in E. Tenn. required of those belonging to the above mentioned class. Those of the E. Tenn. prisoners who communicated state that they are unaware of having violated the laws of the State of Tenn. or those of the C.S., profess their willingness to live under the Gov. Some have taken the oath of allegiance and all profess themselves willing to do so.*

The first group noted by Carter as taking "the oath in Alabama" and "now confined among the prisoners of war" included three men from Hancock and Hawkins area:

- M. Hurly, Hancock, is believed to be Moses Hurley, age sixty-eight, a resident of Sneedville, District Six of Hancock County.
- J. Levisy, Hancock, is believed to be one of two John Levicys living in the War Gap area in the Levicy District of Hancock County.
- J. Goad, Hawkins County.

The second group identified as "willing to take the oath of allegiance" included the following Hancock and Hawkins men:

- I.W. Berry, Hawkins County.

- E.S. McGinnis, Hawkins, identified as E.S. McGinnes, age twenty-five, of Lee Valley, District Two of Hawkins County.
- M.F. Murrell, Hawkins, identified as Martin Murrel, age nineteen, of Lee Valley, Hawkins County.
- W.B. Hurley, Hawkins County.
- W.D. Cobb, Hawkins, believed to be Winstered Cobb, age forty-four, living in Lee Valley, District Two, Hawkins County.
- Thos. Johnson, Hawkins, believed to be Thomas Johnson, living in Lee Valley, Hawkins County.
- Jno. Waddle, Hancock, identified as John Waddle, age twenty, of War Creek, Holland District of Hancock County.
- Wm. Goins, Hancock, believed to be Wm. Goens, age eighteen, of War Creek in the Murrel District of Hancock County.

Just as significant are the Hancock and Hawkins men that Carter failed to mention or include on his list of those returning from Tuscaloosa, such as Ephraim Byrd, N. Hurley, believed to be Nehemiah Harley and Jacob Myers (identified as Jacob Myars in the census). Exactly what happened to these men is unknown. Did they die while in prison at Tuscaloosa, escape or continue to be incarcerated at the Alabama prison and were then later released?

A present-day park located in downtown Tuscaloosa, Alabama, near the old Tuscaloosa Confederate prison site. *Courtesy of the author's collection.*

Regardless of the verdicts and imprisonments handed down by the East Tennessee Confederate District Court during its 1862 winter session, authorities only condemned seven bridge burners, with five ultimately going to the gallows. The court allowed many more to go free after taking the oath of loyalty, while forcing others into service of the Confederate army. But possibly a greater number, between two hundred and four hundred offenders, like Ephraim Byrd, whose crimes authorities considered more serious due to activities in Union militias, were placed on train cars and sent to the Confederate prison in Tuscaloosa, Alabama, where some no doubt lingered and died.

Tuscaloosa, one of the earliest POW prisons established by the Rebels, was strategically located deep in the heart of the Confederacy. Prisoners sent from Knoxville and east Tennessee that fall and winter of 1861–1862 ultimately mingled with other Union prisoners, many captured at the First Bull Run, the first major battle of the war in July 1861. Confederates confined the Tuscaloosa prisoners in warehouses at the foot of River Hill in two two-story brick buildings in the town's business district, all of which constituted the prison facility. Interestingly, the infamous Sergeant Henry Wirz commanded the Tuscaloosa prison for a brief period early in the war. Wirz became the only man hanged by the Federal government for war crimes; in fact, his war crimes trial in late 1865 is reputed to have been the first such trial in U.S. history. His execution resulted from the oversight of the notorious Andersonville prison in Georgia late in the war, not the Tuscaloosa prison.[137]

CHAPTER 8

Profile of a Raiding Party

The exact persons and groups who perpetuated the deadly confrontation on that fateful December day will probably never be fully known, but sufficient information survives, implicating several individuals who had direct personal involvement or strong influence in formulating the attack. It is admitted that some of this information would be found lacking if held to modern legal standards, with some of it based more on accusation rather than hard evidence. As far as we know, no one has been tried or found guilty of killing Captain William K. Byrd or any of his militia. Even so, the information that follows comes from some of the most respected Union men of the Civil War period, such as Oliver P. Temple, Crawford W. Hall and William G. Brownlow. They were esteemed men who lived and wrote during this period and personally knew or had acquaintance with many of the principal figures of that era in east Tennessee.

To begin with, of the men suspected of involvement or providing influence in the Byrd raid, none had more prominence than Joseph Brown Heiskell, a resident of Rogersville at the time and a native east Tennessean. Heiskell was born in Knoxville about 1823, the son of Frederick S. Heiskell and Eliza Brown. Joseph's father was an early day newspaperman and, for a time, editor of the *Knoxville Register*. Before the war while living in Madisonville, Tennessee, Joseph took up the practice of law before moving to Rogersville. Elected in 1858 to the Tennessee legislature, Heiskell served faithfully until 1861. About five months after Tennessee's secession, he became a member of the first Confederate Congress.[138]

Joseph Brown Heiskell, ultrasecessionist and Confederate congressman, whom Oliver Temple called an extremist due to his views on Unionists. *Courtesy of the McClung Historical Collection.*

Like many secessionists, Heiskell supported the Whig party and at first opposed secession until Abraham Lincoln's call for volunteers after Fort Sumter. In the summer of 1861, before his election to the Confederate Congress, he tried running for a spot in the Provisional Confederate Congress from the First District but lost to Unionist Thomas A.R. Nelson. Soon after, the Tennessee legislature regerrymandered the state, diluting Unionist voting power, thereby setting up another election in November 1861. This time, Heiskell won a seat to the First Confederate Congress, convening in February 1862. In that congress, Heiskell proved to be one of the most dedicated and active members, rarely missing a vote and offering a number of bills in support of the Davis administration. He voted in favor of two conscription bills and the suspension of the habeas corpus writ. One of his most controversial proposals was his suggestion on September 10, 1862, of creating "a policy of taking hostages in reprisal for the capture and

Judge Oliver P. Temple, an outspoken opponent of secession before the war, later became a moderate voice for Unionism during the war, while providing legal defense for Loyalists. *Courtesy of the W.A. Wicks Album, McClung Historical Collection.*

imprisonment of Southern citizens and other noncombatants." He wanted to arrest any Unionist, no matter how prominent, and hold them as hostage "for their adhesion to the anti-slavery, black republican, anti-Christian government in Washington" until Confederates could be exchanged. Heiskell is later reelected to the Second Confederate Congress, opening in 1864, where he offered additional pieces of legislation.[139]

According to Oliver P. Temple in his book *East Tennessee and the Civil War*, during the period of 1861–1862, nearly every prominent citizen of east Tennessee was extremely bitter and intense in their feelings toward Union people. Moreover, Temple included Joseph Heiskell and two other east Tennessee Confederate congressman, William G. Swan and William H. Tibbs, in this extremist group of prominent citizens. Speaking specifically of Heiskell, Temple stated Heiskell "though still a young man…was an eminent lawyer" but, for unknown reasons, "become extreme in his views and feeling" toward Union people once the war started.

Still referring to Heiskell and the other men, Temple noted that, against Union people, "there could be no line of policy adopted, however severe, that did not meet their approval." They "were intense in their condemnation of the course of Union people." As a result "they were looked to by [Confederate] authorities at Richmond for information and advice as to the course" of handling Union people. Temple stated "their policy of pacification meant banishment or imprisonment." With these men, and others like them, the crime of being or having been a Union man could not be condoned. Union people in their minds were "traitors and tories" to be dealt with severely.[140]

Temple's description of this extremist viewpoint is supported by an article in the *Knoxville Whig* newspaper of August 8, 1866, written by William G. Brownlow, governor of Tennessee (having been elected in March of 1865), which brought more incriminating accusations against Joseph Brown Heiskell.[141] Offering stronger comments than Temple, Brownlow stated in his own passionate, fiery writing style "that Heiskell was a member of the Richmond control, who advocated with great zeal, every severe measure for the punishment of Union men in East Tennessee, which leaded to their subjugation and humiliation." Brownlow further stated that Heiskell was writer and signer of a "bloody petition" to President Davis to adopt more rigid measures against Union men, "calling for the execution of leaders, by way of example." The "bloody petition" mentioned by Brownlow is a likely reference to Heiskell's proposal of taking hostages in reprisal.

William G. "Parson" Brownlow's gravestone and burial plot is located in the Old Gray Cemetery in Knoxville, Tennessee. The cemetery is named for English poet Thomas Gray. *Courtesy of the author's collection.*

Brownlow also described Heiskell as "a man of many talents, who exerted a large influence for evil." Brownlow accused Heiskell of being in the Byrd raid and being "charged with tying up and shooting of poor old Bird full of bullet holes." In addition, Brownlow accused Heiskell of involvement in other Rebel raiding parties in east Tennessee, such as the Chimney Top raid where "he took a prominent role in seeking to kill, wound, and capture" Union men. Brownlow concluded by stating that Heiskell had participated in the Brooks Ferry raid in Hawkins County, where he stood accused of taking shots at his own neighbors.[142]

Along with Heiskell's possible influence and involvement, another reputed leader in the Byrd raid was a man named Bynum, mentioned in Crawford W. Hall's book and thought to be John Gray Bynum. Less renowned than Heiskell, Bynum and his wife, Nancy, before the war lived in the New Canton or District Six area of Hawkins County. A lawyer and Union supporter, Hall referred to Bynum and his gang of Confederate sympathizers as a bunch of "patriotic volunteers in the cause of treason." Without hesitation, Hall stated that Bynum was "the leader of the Byrd raid."[143]

John Gray Bynum and his father-in-law, Joshua Phipps, a farmer, were probably two of the richest men in upper east Tennessee at the time, with Phipps having a combined wealth of "real estate and personal assets" of $100,000 and Bynum's at $140,000, at least according to information from the 1860 census. It's conceivable Bynum could have used his financial status to influence and organize the Byrd raid. But after the war, the Hawkins County Circuit Court grand jury convened in October 1865 to investigate

John D. Riley, Rogersville resident and Southern supporter. *Courtesy of the Kyle Collection.*

Byrd's murder, failing to mention or include Bynum's name or legal representative on the indictment. It is presumed Bynum's untimely death at the hands of another Rebel, John D. Riley, on the streets of Rogersville on December 15, 1862, accounted for Bynum being excluded from those postwar proceedings. The remaining men suspected of strong involvement in the Byrd raid included John W. Phillips, age thirty-four, a merchant before the war who lived at War Gap in far northern Hawkins County. In addition to Phillips, there was also Joseph Huffmaster, age twenty-three, a lawyer and son of Joseph Huffmaster Sr., a seventy-nine-year-old cabinet maker from Rogersville, and Robert Simpson, age forty-one, a former merchant who lived in Mooresburg, a small Hawkins County community located a short distance west of Rogersville.

So in summary, one source had Bynum leading the Byrd raid, while another strongly implicated Captain John W. Phillips and officers of E Company, while still a third accused Joseph Brown Heiskell of serious involvement. Fortunately, this mystery of who actually led the raid was clarified a few years after the war, when Byrd family members and several Hancock County residents provided convincing testimony in Hancock County Chancery Court. This testimony, while not immediately implicating Joseph Brown Heiskell directly in the raid, left little doubt as to one of the raid's leaders and several of its participants. It clearly pointed to Captain John W. Phillips and the men of Company E, Forty-third Tennessee Infantry, CSA.

The testimony implicating Phillips appeared in the case of *William Trent v. Robert Kyle and John Phillips*, a Hancock County Chancery Court proceeding on August 7–17, 1868, involving a land dispute.[144] This particular action, according to chancery court papers, started soon after the war's conclusion in 1865 and continued into 1871. While not a criminal court proceeding, several persons, including two sons of the deceased Captain Byrd, Andrew J and William E. Byrd, testified for the plaintiff regarding the character and person of John W. Phillips. Referring to Phillips, Byrd's son Andrew stated,

"He was about taking up men and putting them in the army, he and his men killed my father, he was in the raid that hung some men, and carried off others to prison, some of which died there." Andrew, while not certain of the number of men killed in the raid, did state "some 4 or 5 were killed. Eidson was said to be in charge of the company at the time." The man Eidson is thought to be Larkin W. Eidson, initially a second lieutenant and later possibly a first lieutenant in Company E, Forty-third Tennessee Infantry, CSA. Larkin, along with being named a codefendant in Byrd's murder, also appears on a second 1865 murder indictment in Hawkins County, relating to a William N. Stapleton. The mere presence of Eidson on two separate murder indictments does seem to suggest a pattern of lawlessness or overt subversive activity by him and members of his unit.

Andrew's testimony initially connected Phillips to the raid, but he later admitted not knowing if Phillips was along. On the other hand, William E. Byrd had his own statements regarding Phillips, but unlike his brother, he testified regarding Phillips, saying, "I have no doubt he was along when Capt. Byrd was killed, and others taken off and put in prison and some of them died there." William also stated that Phillips's men did "nothing else but raid over the countryside."[145] A few days later, on August 14 and 17, as part of the same chancery court proceedings, another man, Malon Anderson testified "it was his understanding that Phillips and his company killed him [Capt. Byrd], about the time the rebels hung John Wiett [*sic*]."

In addition to Anderson, two other men named Samuel Eidson and Nelson G. Seal may have provided the most incriminating testimony connecting Phillips to the Byrd raid. Samuel stated that he heard Captain Phillips "say he was along on the Byrd raid," and after capturing Byrd, he "turned the wounded Byrd over to his Lieutenant [either Joseph Huffmaster or Larkin W. Eidson] who had him shot."

This wasn't the first time someone had accused Huffmaster of having a key role in the affair. A reader's editorial published in the *Knoxville Whig*, dated December 14, 1864, by a person named "Justice" had the following comments regarding Joseph Huffmaster, now a captain:

> *It has been rumored that Capt. Joseph Hoffmaster [sic] was captured by the forces of Gen. Sheridan, near Winchester, Va., two or three months since and that he has been sent North. Capt. Hoffmaster [sic] under the rebel training of his uncle, Major Hord, became not only a traitor but a murderer. It is understood that he was the officer who detailed a squad of men to murder old man Bird, of Hancock County. Such a man ought never*

to be exchanged as a prisoner of war, but should be made an example of, and suffer the just punishment of his crime. Can you inform your readers whether Captain Hoffmaster [sic] has yet been indicted? Is he not a subject for presentment by the Grand Jury?[146]

The writer above is believed to be Alfred Justice of Greene County, Tennessee, a Union sympathizer and scout for the Union army.

Another key witness in the chancery court proceedings, Nelson G. Seal of Hancock County, testified that Phillips and his men came to his house on Sunday, December 8, 1861, a day after the raid and told Seal they had killed William Byrd. Seal also testified that Byrd, a grandfather, "was considered a peaceable and mild man." Seal further stated that the surrounding community feared Phillips and his men. This was due in part to Phillips having left, according to Seal, a contingent of his raiding party behind, with an apparent mission to patrol, seek out and arrest suspected Unionists in the area.[147] Seal, according to the 1860 census, lived in Sixth District of Hancock County, having its post office at Sneedville.[148] Other persons testifying in the same chancery court proceedings and painting similar impressions of John W. Phillips's tarnished character included Hiram Herd, Sarah Jane Trent, Thomas E. Herd, Nelson Stapleton, Jack Buttery, William Seal, William B. Davis and John Herd.[149]

Of those who testified for the plaintiff, the most surprising seemed to be Samuel Eidson and his apparent willingness to even testify at all. Samuel, himself a Confederate veteran, had enlisted in October 1862 for service with Company F, Sixteenth Tennessee Cavalry Battalion, CSA, only to become a deserter by December 1864. Even more so, Samuel should have been discouraged from testifying due the apparent fact that he had at least two, maybe three, brothers with service in Phillips's E Company, Forty-third Infantry—Creton and William Eidson. The third brother appears to be none other than Larkin W., a previously noted E Company member who was initially a second lieutenant and then later possibly, as once source noted, elected a first lieutenant in May 1862 and possibly implicated by testimony of Andrew J. Byrd as "being in charge of the company" the day of the raid.[150] While unknown, Samuel's testimony for the plaintiff may have been a classic situation of "brother against brothers." Granted, it was only a civil proceeding in chancery court in August 1868, but the possible drama as Samuel spoke his incriminating words may have caused a disturbing chill for his brothers and the former Rebels possibly in attendance. Samuel detailed events of a cold and bloody day in December nearly seven years before, offering potentially convicting words some, including his brothers, may have preferred left in the past.

The chancery court record for the complainant goes on to describe a dark time in Hancock County during this 1861–1862 period, one full of fear and oppression while living under Confederate military law. It was a time when Confederates arrested many citizens in Hancock County and surrounding areas, resulting in many being sent off to Southern prisons for their devotion to the Union, with even larger numbers of people being driven from their homes and compelled to take refuge in Kentucky and the Union army. It also details that John W. Phillips "had been quite active and violent and had arrested and sent off a number of men," apparently to prison. Like the personal testimony, the court record reported that Phillips was a member of "a raiding company that kill men and carried off property."[151]

The Forty-third's attack on Byrd and his Unionist militia on the North side of Clinch would not be its last against a Unionist stronghold. A few months after the Byrd raid, on April 7, 1862, a detachment of the Forty-third regiment moved from Greeneville, Tennessee, to the Shelton Laurel area of Madison County, North Carolina, with orders to "put down any illegal organization of men that might be found there." Shelton Laurel, like the North side of Clinch in December 1861, was a hotbed of Unionist activity then and throughout the war. Led by Lieutenant Colonel David M. Key, the Forty-third would make a sweep over three days—April 8–10—through the valley, killing fifteen of the enemy, while suffering three casualties. It's unknown if the Forty-third detachment that participated in the Shelton Laurel engagement included Captain John W. Phillips's E Company.[152]

In addition to John W. Phillips, there are two other members of the E Company, Forty-third Tennessee Infantry, suspected of having more than token involvement in the Byrd raid: Augustus Teague and Isaac "Ike" Fain, the latter being the younger son of Richard and Eliza Rhea Anderson Fain. To begin with, Augustus Teague is thought to be the man Eliza called Gus Fig in her diary. According to Eliza, Gus's name "is associated with the murder of old Mr. Bird, having made the first effective shot at him."[153] Gus's name also appeared as Gus Tegue on the October 1865 Hawkins County grand jury indictment for Captain Byrd's murder. But interestingly, Eliza noted in her diary entry of March 27, 1862, three months after the Byrd raid, that Fig had become a deserter from the Confederate army. Eliza stated that Captain Phillips and son Ike, along with several members of the company, had come home recently to round up Fig and other deserters.

The other suspected raiding party and E Company member is none other than Sgt. Isaac "Ike" Fain, described by one of his descendants as the "fairly hot-headed son of Eliza," who returned to Rogersville after the war only to be arrested on August 20, 1866, by William O. Sizemore while on a train at Russellville attempting to travel to Bristol. After his arrest, authorities incarcerated Ike in the Rogersville jail under a legal capias writ issued by the Hawkins County Circuit Court, accusing him of "being present, aiding and abetting in the murder of old man Wm. Bird during the reign of the rebels." Soon after, Ike's cousin, Sam Fain, and brother, Hiram, made bail for him. Unfortunately for Ike, his legal troubles would not end here but only increase the following year and continue for a period of time.[154]

CHAPTER 9

Meeting at New Market, Tennessee

C ongressman Joseph Brown Heiskell unexpectedly resigned from the First Confederate Congress on February 17, 1864, just days before its conclusion. According to his resignation letter sent to the speaker of the House, Heiskell disapproved of the body's recent handling and lack of overall progress in the "prisoner exchange program," thus motivating his resignation.[155] By then, though, Heiskell had already won a seat in the Second Congress convening in May 1864, having run unopposed for reelection on August 3, 1863, for his east Tennessee First District seat. It appears his resignation from the first congress didn't prevent him from taking a seat in the second.[156]

Later that summer, on August 21, 1864, Union soldiers of the Thirteenth Tennessee Cavalry under the command of Lieutenant Colonel William Ingerton captured Heiskell while on a visit to his home in Rogersville during a recess in the Second Confederate Congress.[157] Ingerton's battalion was part of Colonel John K. Miller's Third Brigade, under the command of Union brigadier general Alvan C. Gillem. Ingerton had reached the ford on the Holston at McKinney's Mill just before daylight on August 21, while capturing Confederate pickets stationed nearby in the process. Then, almost as quickly, Ingerton continued on into Rogersville, only three miles distance, where he surprised the small Confederate force.[158]

A brief account of the Rogersville raid is given by Confederate B. Franklin Allison, member of Company C, Sixty-third Tennessee Infantry, CSA. Allison, for several weeks prior, had been engaged in rounding up absentee members

Brigadier General Alvan C. Gillem was born a Southerner but remained loyal. He led several Union campaigns in east Tennessee late in the war; one involved surprising and killing Confederate general John H. Morgan at Greeneville, Tennessee, in September 1864. *Courtesy of Library of Congress.*

from his regiment living in Sullivan and Hawkins Counties. As Ingerton's Union troops surrounded the town, Allison stood waiting with a company of Confederate soldiers near the jail where several Union soldiers were prisoners. As a Rebel orderly sergeant announced roll call, Allison said several gunshots rang out, causing the sleepy-eyed and still partially clad Rebel soldiers to scatter for safety, followed closely by Allison. As the men ran, Allison saw one man take a gunshot wound and fall only steps away. Quickly and without warning, the town was surrounded on three sides by blue coats.

Lieutenant Colonel William H. Ingerton, highly respected by his men, survived the Rogersville raid only to die four months later from a gunshot wound inflicted by a ex-federal officer. *Courtesy of Roger D. Hunt Collection at U.S. Army Military History Institute.*

Allison continued running up Depot Street near the present-day Rogersville Courthouse, eventually jumping over a paling fence into the yard of a Mrs. Poats, where Poats suggested that Allison take refuge under her back porch with three other men. One of those men was her husband, a sergeant and fellow member in Allison's company, who was home on leave. To protect the men from discovery, Mrs. Poats threw "an old muddy carpet over the tracks to the hole under her house." As Allison and the others lay quietly, Union lieutenant William Owens searched Mrs. Poats's house and the one next door, where a Colonel Walker, a civilian and elderly man, was caught hiding in the attic. Shortly thereafter, several other suspected Rebels were arrested, including Joseph Brown Heiskell.

As fighting subsided, Federals emptied the jail of Union prisoners, foraged about for food and soon learned of a Confederate force approaching from the east. To counter this threat, Colonel Ingerton made an unsuccessful attempt to get behind the approaching Confederates, only to decide he was up against a superior force. Calling a halt to the raid, Ingerton formed a rear guard, retreated back across the Holston River and rejoined his command. As for Private Allison, thanks to Mrs. Poats and her back porch hiding place, he made good on his escape, but after returning home, he saw his luck run out two days later when he was captured by the same Union regiment.[159]

John Bell Brownlow, son of William G. "Parson" Brownlow and a member of Gillem's Union command at the time of Heiskell's capture, later stated that Heiskell

had been the particeps crimini [an accomplice or accessory] *to the atrocious murder of several Union citizens, and through several counties had accompanied and encouraged a band of rebel bushwhackers and thieves who lacerated with whips the backs of the wives, sisters, and daughters of Union soldiers. Because of these atrocious and inhuman acts it was with difficulty that Gen. Gillem could prevent the outraged Union soldiers of East Tennessee from taking his life.*[160]

Another account of Heiskell's capture is found in the official Union army record in a communication from General Gillem to Andrew Johnson just four days after the daylight raid on Rogersville. According to Gillem's report, the raid resulted in killing twenty-three Rebels and capturing twenty-five, with Joe Heiskell and Colonel Walker (Watkins) among those captured, along with several noncommissioned officers. Gillem closed his dispatch by stating that "Joe Heiskell walked to meet us." Gillem's report to Governor Johnson was passed along to President Lincoln, who quickly responded. Lincoln thanked Gillem and Johnson for the good news and with a bit of satire, asking, "Does Joe Heiskell's 'walking to meet us,' mean any more than that Joe was scared and wanted to save his skin?"[161]

But unlike Lincoln, east Tennessee Unionists undoubtedly harbored no satirical feelings regarding Heiskell's capture. They clearly considered him a dangerous prisoner of war, entitled to the same harsh treatment he had reaped on them, with nothing short of a death sentence fully justified by the most ardent Unionist. Even Andrew Johnson, military governor of Tennessee, soon after the capture of Watkins and Heiskell in correspondence to Union general William Sherman, described the two as "bad men, [who] exercised a dangerous and deleterious influence in the country, and deserve as many deaths as can be inflicted upon them."

Johnson went on to caution Sherman regarding the "political influence" of both men, saying they "are extensively connected with influential persons throughout the region [east Tennessee], and a powerful influence would be brought to bear in favor of releasing them on parole and bonds."

Andrew Johnson knew of the political pressure that would be brought by Heiskell's family and friends to release him. *Courtesy of Tennessee State Library and Archives.*

Johnson closed by recommending the removal of both men from Knoxville as soon as possible.[162]

On one hand, it remains debatable whether Heiskell deserved the harsh treatment and attention demanded by many Unionists following his capture; on the other hand, most observers agree that, considering his position and influence in the Confederate government, Heiskell clearly stood as one of the most highly profiled Rebel civilians or political prisoners taken in east Tennessee during the war. After capture, Union authorities transported Heiskell by train to Knoxville along with several other prisoners, arriving on the evening of August 30.[163] As reported, Federal authorities incarcerated Heiskell at Castle Fox, or Knoxville city jail, the same "hell hole" used by the Rebels to imprison Loyalists less than three years before. At first glance, most Unionists no doubt cheered the extreme circumstances now confronting Heiskell while anticipating his trial for treason. Many may have believed that justice would soon be served on the man so many felt responsible for horrible acts and crimes against Unionists, but appearances can be deceiving. To the contrary, evidence suggests Heiskell received special treatment and protection from Union authorities, beginning possibly with his confinement in Knoxville but definitely with his later imprisonment in Nashville, where Heiskell was isolated and made "comfortable" from the general prison population. While hard to imagine, Joseph Brown Heiskell—the scourge and enemy of so many Unionists—may have never darkened the door of Castle Fox. Rather, it's believed authorities in Knoxville showed Heiskell more accommodating facilities, such as the Bell House hotel or other less intimidating confines than the city jail. But regardless, five weeks later, the military ushered Heiskell off to the city jail at Nashville.

Heiskell arrived in Nashville on October 9, 1864, where Union captain William Hunter Brooks, provost marshal, assumed control of the prisoner. Brooks had a directive from Sherman's headquarters, telling him to hold Heiskell in confinement and await further orders. Less than a week later, on October 14, Captain Brooks received new orders from Major General Thomas, apparently of Sherman's headquarters, ordering Brooks to transmit Heiskell on to the military prison in Nashville. General Thomas also made special effort in the communiqué to tell Brooks to "provide the prisoner with as comfortable quarters as possible, and to keep him [Heiskell] separate from [other] Rebel prisoners."

This apparent special treatment afforded to Heiskell by Union authorities in Nashville likely would have enraged most Unionists in east Tennessee, including Andrew Johnson, if known at the time.[164] Certainly "comfortable

Major General Samuel P. Carter was a graduate of the U.S. Naval Academy in 1846. A brevet major general in the Union army, he returned to the navy after the war and became a rear admiral. *Courtesy of Tennessee State Museum*

quarters" was not what Andrew Johnson had in mind for Heiskell in his letter to General Sherman only days before. Eventually, Heiskell was imprisoned in the North at Camp Chase, Columbus, Ohio.

But while still in Nashville, the wheels within the Confederacy began turning in earnest to obtain Heiskell's freedom. In a memoranda to Union major John E. Mulford dated November 8, 1864, Judge Robert Ould, Confederate agent of exchange, inquired of Heiskell's "state of health." A day later, on November 9, the Confederate office of adjutant general in Richmond, at the order of Secretary of War James Seddon, issued special order No. 267 to Confederate major general J.C. Breckinridge. The order gave Breckinridge power to authorize Brigadier General John C. Vaughn to negotiate with Union military authorities in east Tennessee for the exchange of all political prisoners or noncombatants held on both sides. Along with the broader text, the order specifically mentioned Heiskell by name as one of the prisoners in which Confederate authorities had a particular interest. With focus seemingly on Heiskell, Confederate authorities may have feared future actions by the Union military of turning Heiskell over to the state or civilian courts, as previously done with several other secessionists.

A few days later, while under a flag of truce, Union brigadier general Samuel P. Carter, former general of the Second Tennessee Infantry Regiment, USA, and now provost marshal-general of east Tennessee, met with General Vaughn in New Market, Tennessee, for the purpose of negotiating the release of noncombatants from East Tennessee, as authorized under special order No. 267. During this meeting with Carter, Vaughn placed emphasis on "securing release of persons indicted for treason in the US court for the District of East Tennessee."

But Carter told Vaughn that he was presently forbidden by the U.S. War Department to interfere with those cases. Despite this apparent rejection by Carter, the meeting concluded with Vaughn agreeing to make no further arrests of citizens, except the four already seized as hostages for Joseph B. Heiskell—the direct result of a previous order by Confederate secretary of war James Seddon. Unfortunately, neither Vaughn nor Carter revealed the names of the Union hostages being held in retaliation.[165]

On December 10, 1864, General Vaughn, from his headquarters at Greeneville, Tennessee, reported to Secretary Seddon in Richmond regarding the Carter meeting while also providing a copy of the agreement reached between the two for future prisoner exchanges. The agreement consisted of the following provisions: first, Confederates would release all Tennessee civilian prisoners; second, the Federals would release all persons taken in retaliation for Confederate arrests; third, Carter would try and obtain the release of all Confederate political prisoners; and fourth, both sides would allow persons who had fled their homes to return and live unmolested, provided they remained loyal and observed all laws.

In the same report, Vaughn regretfully confessed his failure to obtain the release of Heiskell and several others indicted for treason. Vaughn told Seddon of General Carter's reassurances and endeavors to do his best to secure the release of Joseph B. Heiskell. Vaughn went on to request the secretary's approval of the prisoner exchange agreement and, if so approved, then show his consent by releasing all Union citizen prisoners currently held in confinement in east Tennessee and sending them to his department as soon as possible. Vaughn closed his report asking the secretary if he disapproved of the arrangement, and whether he would be willing for Vaughn to arrest additional prominent Union men as hostages for Heiskell.[166]

A few days later, on December 15, Secretary Seddon, in a strongly worded response to General Vaughn regarding the December 10 report, voiced disapproval of the prisoner exchange agreement hammered out with Carter. Referring to the agreement, Seddon pointed out that while all "Union citizens of East Tennessee who are held by Confederate authorities shall be released, there is no corresponding stipulation in respect to our own loyal people," especially in regard to those arrested in east Tennessee and turned over to the state for indictment—persons whom Seddon called in "hopeless captivity," which Carter agreed only "to use his best efforts" to gain release.[167] As result, Seddon said those Union men arrested earlier by Rebels in retaliation would therefore remain hostages for their people. Seddon concluded by telling Vaughn that if he was unable "to secure general citizen prisoners belonging to East Tennessee, including Mr. Heiskell," he would approve Vaughn's former request "to arrest a number of [additional] prominent men as hostages."[168] It is unknown what other citizens, if any, were subsequently arrested by Vaughn. But despite this initial rejection by Secretary Seddon, the prisoner exchange agreement crafted by Carter and Vaughn did result in a number of prisoners being exchanged by both sides.

Beginning in early December, Vaughn notified Carter of twenty-nine prisoners being sent to Union lines. In turn, Carter released several hostages and notified Vaughn with a list of those persons. Carter also sent a copy of the exchange agreement to Major General Ethan Allan Hitchcock, Union commissioner for exchange, asking Hitchcock to send all east Tennessee Confederate political prisoners at Camp Chase and Johnson's Island to Knoxville. This latter action resulted in several more civilian prisoners being released by early February 1865; noticeably missing from those released was one man, Confederate congressman Joseph Brown Heiskell, who remained in prison at Camp Chase.[169]

While these prisoner exchanges in east Tennessee showed limited success, the whole process broke down in early 1865, with both sides accusing the other of bad faith and broken promises. In a memoranda dated February 20, 1865, to Union brigadier general L.S. Trowbridge, who by this time had succeeded Carter as provost marshal-general of east Tennessee, General Vaughn recounted his oral promise to General Carter in the New Market meeting to show restraint in making further arrests on behalf of Joseph B. Heiskell. Vaughn told Trowbridge, due to Heiskell's continued confinement, he had "given orders for the further arrest of citizens to hold as hostages for him [Heiskell]."

Vaughn closed this communication to Trowbridge by giving his "solemn assurance that whenever a proper disposition shall be exhibited by U.S. authorities to carry out the letter and spirit of our agreement" from the New Market meeting, which only could be achieved by releasing "all citizens prisoners now in custody and ceasing to make such arrests in the future," then—and only then—would Vaughn discharge all Union prisoners held by their side.[170]

This attempt at prisoner exchange, ongoing since the previous fall, effectively ended on March 2, 1865, when Secretary Seddon notified General Vaughn that a national agreement had been reached for exchange of all civilian prisoners. As a consequence, Tennessee civilian prisoners would no longer be sent to Vaughn but exchanged elsewhere.

Along with the efforts by General Vaughn and Carter, Heiskell's personal friends and political cronies also worked in tandem to free him from Federal prison. In November 1864, fellow Confederate congressman and childhood friend William G. Swan, with supporting letters, wrote President Davis on Heiskell's behalf, pleading for help. The accompanying letters from Swan to President Davis related the "circumstances attending the arrest and subsequent treatment of my colleague in the House" and the "cruelties and indignities to which he is subjected."

Along with Swan's letter, several other members of the Confederate Tennessee congressional delegation in January 1865 wrote yet another letter to Davis, this time proposing that General Robert E. Lee be allowed to approach General Ulysses S. Grant regarding a trade of Heiskell for Grant's brother-in-law, John Dent, who at the time was a Rebel prisoner.[171]

In a letter dated March 11, 1865, to President Jefferson Davis, Confederate agent of exchange judge Robert Ould related Grant's apparent answer when approached about trading Dent for Heiskell. Ould indicated Grant ignored his personal relationship with Dent by rejecting the plan, stating "that Dent was a disloyal [Union] man, known to him as such, and that he would not do as much for him as he would for any other citizen prisoner."

Ould told President Davis that he had waited a long time to be able to tell him something positive and "decisive in the case of Mr. Heiskell," but Federal authorities had either refused or made little or no reply to his many communications. However, Ould promised to "press the case" with the Federals.[172]

Ultimately these efforts by Confederate authorities and Heiskell's friends to shorten his prison sentence met with little or no apparent success. Heiskell remained in prison until the end of the war, thereupon being paroled by order of Union secretary of war Edwin M. Stanton in June 1865.[173]

CHAPTER 10

Indictments for Murder
and Treason

Afurther his release from prison, Joseph Brown Heiskell returned to Rogersville, only to be warned to leave town by local Unionists. Soon after, Joseph and brother Carrick, a Confederate veteran, apparently took the hint and relocated to Memphis.[174] In August 1865, two sons of Captain William K. Byrd, Andrew J. and William E., initiated a legal suit in the Hawkins County Circuit Court for a violation of "trespass," which amounted to a civil action for compensation in the case of *Andrew J. Byrd admin. of the William Byrd dec.d v. George Moore, W. S. Creed and Others.* Initially, the trespass action included Joseph Heiskell's name, along with several other defendants. But barely two months later, on October 4, 1865, the Hawkins County court reported that Heiskell was inexplicably dismissed or dropped from Andrew's suit with no apparent explanation. The court entry simply stated that "the plaintiff, [Andrew J. Byrd] dismisses his suit as to the defendant Joseph B. Heiskell," with judgment against Byrd levied for Heiskell's expenses in the suit.

Later that same month, a Hawkins County Circuit Court grand jury voted on a bill of indictment against fifty-one men for the murder of William K. Byrd, in the *State v. John Phillips and Larkin Eidson, et al.*[175] (See the Appendix A for a copy of the Byrd murder indictment.) It appears this grand jury had been in session for several weeks leading up to the indictment, investigating various crimes and claims evolving from the war. Like the civil action started by the Byrd family in circuit court for the violation of trespass, the murder indictment initially included Joseph Heiskell's name.

Hawkins County Courthouse. Completed in 1837, this view is from July 1998. Much of the legal action for the Byrd Raid took place here. *Courtesy of the author's collection.*

The October 1865 Hawkins County murder indictment listed the following men: John Phillips, Larkin Eidson, George Moore, John D. Riley, Swimpfield Anderson, Henry S. Wax, Larkin W. Kyle, Barnett Cantwell, Joseph B. Heiskell, Eli Cox, James Grantens, Hiram Mills, David McCoy, Daniel S, McCulley, Hiram K. Riley, William S. Rose, Jacob Miller, Thomas Moore, Calvin Jones, Abijah Anderson, George Anderson, Hiram Tucker, Christian Tucker, Elbert Day, Westley Moore, Zackariah Biggs, Jessie T. Leirsey (Livesay), Gus Tegue (Augustus Teague), John Baker, Josiah Lawson, Woodson Wolf, Pleasant Walker, John Brooks, James Zink (Jink?), David Cantwell, Joseph Huffmaster, Swimpfield Eidson, George Martin, Moses Anderson, Isaah Fain (believed to be Isaac or "Ike" Fain), John Cantwell, James Forrester, Henry Rose, James Long, William Moore, James Kyle, Christopher Kyle, Stephen Thompson, Lipscome Parrott, James Long (may be duplicated) Calvin Baker and Abijah Manis.

Of those indicted, the following thirty-four are believed to be members of the Confederate sympathizer group led by the man Crawford W. Hall identified as Bynum, who is believed to be John Gray Bynum. This "sympathizer group" consisted of civilian men found unconnected from any recognized or known Confederate military unit, at least leading up to the first week of December 1861. This subgroup included: John D Riley, Swimpfield Anderson, Henry S. Wax, Barnett Cantwell, Eli Cox, James Grantens, Hiram Mills, David McCoy, Daniel S. McCulley, Hiram K. Riley, William S. Rose, Thomas Moore, Abijah Anderson, Christian Tucker, Elbert Day, Westley Moore, Woodson Wolf, Pleasant Walker, John Brooks, James Zink (Jink?), David Cantwell, Jesse T. Livesay, Swimpfield Eidson (Eidson and Livesay would later join the Sixteenth Tennessee Cavalry Battalion, CSA), Moses Anderson, John Cantwell (both Anderson and Cantwell later served),

James Forrester, James Long (Long may be duplicated on the indictment list), William Moore, Libscome Parrott, Calvin Baker, George Anderson, Stephen Thompson, Christopher Kyle and James Kyle.

Of the remaining seventeen indicted, official records showed at least ten being documented members of Company E, Forty-third Tennessee Infantry, with one man, Colonel Joseph B. Heiskell, strongly suspected of acting in a senior leadership role at the time of the raid: Joseph B. Heiskell, John Phillips, Larkin Eidson, John Baker, Zackariah Biggs, Isaah Fain (Isaac or "Ike"), Joseph Huffmaster, Josiah Lawson, Abijah Manis, Gus Tegue (listed as Augustus Teague on the Forty-third roster) and Calvin Jones (Calvin Janis in the 1860 census).

Of the remaining six in the above group, they represented or had membership in several different Confederate companies other than Company E, Forty-third Tennessee Infantry, at the time of the raid: George Moore, Larkin W. Kyle, Jacob Miller, Hiram Tucker, George Martin and Henry Rose.

Upon further analysis, using 1860 census and Hawkins County military records, at least nineteen of the fifty-one men indicted in October 1865—or nearly 40 percent—can be reliably identified as living near War Gap of District Three, Hawkins County, an area that bordered on the Hawkins and Hancock boundary line. Such notables on the indictment list were Captain John W. Phillips, Larkin W. Eidson and Gus Tegue, as well as all four Andersons who lived in War Gap. Phillips, a War Gap merchant, and possibly Larkin W. Eidson, a farmer, represented two very key members in E Company in the suspected raiding party leadership.

Of the Andersons living at War Gap, the first included Abijah Anderson, age fifty-four, a fairly well-to-do farmer; George Anderson, likely a brother to Abijah; Moses Anderson, relationship unknown; and Swindfield Anderson, age seventy-eight, born in Virginia and possibly father of the others. The elder Anderson, according to court records, died shortly after the war apparently of natural causes. The other notable was Gus Tegue, a War Gap resident and thirty-year-old farm laborer who lived with the John Pope family. Eliza Fain identified Tegue in her diary as making the "first effective shot" on Byrd.[176]

In addition to Larkin W. Eidson, several other Eidson family members lived in the War Gap area; they included brothers Creton and William Eidson, who later in 1862 would enlist in their brother's Company E, Forty-third Tennessee, CSA. But neither Creton nor William received indictments from the Hawkins grand jury or specific mention in the Hancock County Chancery Court proceedings, which might allow one to conclude that neither man had a role or presence during the raid that fateful December day. The remaining War Gap raiders lived nearby or in adjoining areas, across the townships of Levicy, Wallen and Click of Hancock County but with all listing War Gap, Hawkins County, as their post office.

From all indications, War Gap–area residents on both sides of the county line made up a hotbed of Rebel sympathies and secessionist activities in late 1861. Considering Hancock and Hawkins Counties, no other area seemed to have contributed more support for the raid on Byrd than War Gap. The War Gap Rebels lived only a short ride, maybe less than an hour in some cases, from either group of Unionist Byrds at Lee Valley or War Creek, making the fight with Byrd a classic civil war—neighbor against neighbor.

Along with the Rebel contingent at War Gap, there were as many as ten other indicted Rebels who lived in the War Creek area of Hancock County, no doubt closer to the Byrds at War Creek than those at Lee Valley or War Gap. This group included the Cantwell family, Barnett, David and John, living in the Murrel District, with Barnett, age fifty-one, the likely senior member and fairly well-to-do farmer who had income and property of $12,000, according to 1860 census. Barnett's family included two sons, David, age sixteen, and John, age nineteen, with John possibly later serving in Company E of Ashby's Second Tennessee Cavalry, CSA. In addition to possible involvement by the Barnett Cantwell family, another Cantwell family lived nearby in the Holland District of Hancock, a David Cantwell, age forty-nine, and two sons, Barnet, age eighteen, and John, age fourteen. Both Cantwell families lived in close proximity and possessed similar first names, making it highly probable they represented two branches of the same family. Unfortunately, this same reason of similar first names precluded accurate identifications of exactly which three of the six Cantwells were accused of participation in the Byrd raid.

Along with the Cantwells, other Rebel supporters on the indictment living in the War Creek area included: James Jinks, age forty-five; David McCoy, age fifty-four; Hiram Mills, age fifty-three; Hiram Tucker, who may have served in Company E of Ashby's Tennessee Cavalry, CSA; Pleasant Walker, age twenty-three; Woodson Wolf, age twenty-seven (and possibly Woods or Wiley Wolf in the census); and James Grantens, age thirty-nine (possibly James Gorden in the census). Also, between the Cantwells and the others, all listed themselves as farmers in the census and possessing enough income to make them seem fairly well-to-do, with several holding substantial money and land holdings.

As far as the remaining or smaller group of six men, they were enrolled with other Confederate military units at the time of the raid. They included one of two George Moores, as noted in the 1860 Hawkins County census, who may be the same George Moore who served in Company E of Ashby's Second Tennessee Cavalry, CSA. Another man, Hiram Tucker, can't be accurately identified due there being two Hiram Tuckers living in Hancock County at the time of the raid, with one serving in the same company as George Moore. As far as Larkin W. Kyle, it appears he served like George Moore in Ashby's Second, but with C Company. As far as Jacob Miller, it's very possible this individual had connections to or possibly led the Hawkins County Confederate sympathizer group known as the Beech Creek Jerkers. But again, any connection can't be confirmed due to the existence of at least four Jacob Millers in the 1860 Hawkins census. Lastly, George Martin of the War Gap area and Henry Rose of Sneedville both appear enrolled at the time of the raid with Company K, Nineteenth Tennessee Infantry, CSA.

In late October 1865, authorities in Rogersville responded to the Hawkins murder indictment, attempting to use a "murder-warrant procedure" in an effort to bring Joseph Heiskell back from Memphis. A deputy from Rogersville traveled to Memphis with a legal capias writ issued by the Hawkins court, ordering Heiskell's arrest, only to be thwarted by an intervening local judge who was sympathetic to Heiskell. Local Shelby County sheriff P.M. Winters actually arrested Heiskell on November 10, 1865, but the following day, West Memphis Criminal Court judge Lovick P. Jones entered the fray. Taking control of the situation, Judge Jones responded to a writ of habeas corpus, apparently written by Heiskell himself, testing the legality of his arrest. In his plea to Judge Jones, Heiskell stated, if not unjustly, of being "illegally restrained of his liberty" by Sheriff Winters due to the "alleged indictment for murder" from the Hawkins County Circuit Court. Heiskell repudiated any guilt in the Hawkins murder and asked to be placed under custody of Judge Jones. The writ closed with a promise by Heiskell to appear "at such time and place as his Honor may direct, that he may make returns of the cause against him."

Later that same day, November 11, without further evidence or pleas from Heiskell or authorities, Judge Jones issued an order to Sheriff Winters, commanding Heiskell's appearance at his court. The judge's order stated that Heiskell had been "unlawfully detained" and the matter would now be "dealt with according to law," presumably by Judge Jones. Complying, Sheriff Winters released Heiskell, thus ending Heiskell's brief overnight stay in confinement. Once free and under the power of Judge Jones, Heiskell received bail and temporary freedom, bonding out at $5,000 and giving his agreement to appear at the next term of the Hawkins County Court in January 1866 to answer the charges against him. Three of Heiskell's friends, W.Y.C. Humes, H.E. Jackson and Wm. K. Poston helped provide security on the bail bond. Both Humes and Jackson were former members of the Confederate military.[177]

According to Hawkins County Court records, this legal battle between Joseph Heiskell and Hawkins County authorities, intent on his apprehension, was waged for nearly two years. While avoiding arrest with help from Judge Jones, Heiskell ultimately broke his promise, along with his three supporters, by failing to appear at the January 1866 term of the Hawkins court. Consequently, on February 6, 1866, the Hawkins court ruled Joseph Heiskell and the others in "default" of their $5,000 bond, therefore subjecting it to possible forfeiture to the state of Tennessee, "unless they show good and sufficient cause to the contrary" by the May term of the court. This order, like the one in November, eventually ended up in the hands of Shelby County sheriff P.M. Winters.

On April 30, 1866, Memphis deputy sheriff J.F. Lunsford served Heiskell and the others, but it's unclear whether any of the men, including Heiskell, were taken into custody at the time. What is known took place a few days later on May 10, when Sheriff Winters attempted to take Heiskell into custody but was prevented from doing so by local U.S. marshal M.T. Ryder. Ryder of west Tennessee told Winters he had orders from the local U.S. circuit court to hold Heiskell on treason charges and refused to deliver him. Once again, for the second time in six months, Heiskell escaped custody on the Hawkins County charges. Whether these succeeding episodes were part of some ruse or plot by authorities to protect Heiskell's skin is unknown. But both actions to obviously protect Heiskell seemed to infer that the Rebel congressman still wielded considerable influence and personal sway despite any detrimental impact the war may have had in his political or personal well-being. His work in politics in the state legislature before the war and later in the Confederate government no doubt left him with many friends, political connections and a host of "friends in high places" more than willing to assist or offer second chances.

At long last, on October 2, 1866, in the Hawkins circuit court, Joseph Heiskell, along with his bond supporters and represented by their attorneys, responded to Hawkins authorities. The document presented at that time by the party's defense team noted that the writ or order pending against Heiskell and "the judgment on which it was founded, are not sufficient in law." Heiskell's attorneys went on to cite what appears to be three minor technicalities involving the bonding and appearance processes, with none of it pertaining to Heiskell's possible innocence or charges pending against him.

In January 1867, while continuing to spar back and forth, the Hawkins circuit court issued a third summons for Joseph Heiskell's arrest that was once again delivered by Sheriff Winters of Shelby County. But like the two previous summonses, it ended with the same song, different verse. Sheriff Winters attempted to serve the order on April 24, 1867, only to be frustrated by another U.S. marshal, this time officer Sam Jones, who claimed custody of Heiskell.[178] In the end, this legal maneuvering of nearly two years accomplished nothing as far as getting Heiskell back in Rogersville to face murder charges. On the other hand, Heiskell's efforts and those of his attorneys and friends likely kept him out of jail and away from a possible death sentence. In fact, the delays caused by the repeated legal actions became Heiskell's biggest ally in his personal defense. A treason or death conviction, conceivable during the height of the radical Republican period, 1864 to 1868, all but became impossible to obtain as time went on. Furthermore, with decline of Republican radical political power coming near the end of the 1860s, Heiskell's freedom no longer seemed doubtful. This fact was no better evident than in Heiskell's own situation, where his name, initially part of both the 1865 Hawkins County murder indictment and Andrew Byrd's trespass actions, is found missing inexplicably from both processes by 1868. Granted, other unknown legal maneuvering behind the scenes could have caused this result. Or it may have resulted from sheer frustration or hopelessness of the suing parties, brought on partly by the obvious failure of Hawkins County legal authorities to ultimately arrest or put the legal clamps on Heiskell.

The grand jurors who brought the October 1865 Byrd murder indictment included William Sizemore, Stokely D. Trent, Lucinda Burton, Nancy Curry, James Davis, George W. Huntsman, John B. Proffitt (Phophet?), E. Sievary (Livesay?), David Sovens (Lovens?) and Fredrick Brenen (Brennen?). James Brittain (Britton?) signed the indictment. Interestingly, of the eleven grand jurors, Confederates had arrested Stokely D. Trent back in late 1861, which resulted in Trent's imprisonment and appearance before the East Tennessee District Court in Knoxville and eventual release in January 1862. Juror Nancy Curry, wife of John Curry, would years later—after her husband's death—marry Captain Byrd's son, William E. Byrd, in 1895.[179] Also, Juror James Brittain may be the same James Britton Jr. who was

William O. Sizemore enlisted with the South but later became leader of a lawless band of Unionist guerrillas. He served on the grand jury that brought the Byrd murder indictment in October 1865. *Courtesy of Haynes Alvis, Rogersville, Tn.*

arrested back in mid-November 1861 at Lick Springs in Greene County.[180] Britton, identified by Rebel authorities of "floating" between Greene, Hawkins and Washington Counties, was arrested for using "seditious and incendiary language." Lastly, the jury panel included William Sizemore; the notorious guerrilla leader and undoubtedly the most infamous of the group. William O., or Bill as many called him, served as a law officer in Rogersville and owned a local hotel as well. Bill would later die from a revenge killing by Irodell Willis on October 11 1867. Willis had served as one of Bill's chief aids during their guerrilla days.[181]

The Hawkins County murder indictment resulted in summonses being served on each man with a bond of $10,000, but records indicate only a few actually were served. Most ended up being returned by the local sheriff or law officer with various explanations: "can't locate, has moved, or no longer lives in this County." Also, despite the attention and publicity the indictment may have had, it appears Eliza's son, Isaac "Ike" Fain, in 1866 and Joseph Heiskell in 1865 were the only persons known to have been arrested and jailed for their suspected involvement in the raid and death of

William K. Byrd.[182] None of the other principals in the raid, such as John W. Phillips, Larkin W. Eidson, Gus Teague (Gus Fig) or Joseph Huffmaster, among others, had to explain their involvement or account for any suspected criminal actions surrounding the Byrd raid.

Along with the above tresspass action and murder indictment by the Hawkins County grand jury, filed in August and October 1865, two other court actions were filed in the summer of 1865, specifically against former captain John W. Phillips in the Hawkins County Circuit Court. The first was filed on July 28 by a John Vaughan, with support from Joseph Wills (Willis?) against Phillips "in which Vaughan claim damages of five thousand dollars for trespass with force and arms." It appears Vaughan and Wills, both fellow Confederates, had served during the war in Company F, Sixteenth Tennessee Cavalry Battalion, CSA.[183] It's not known what prompted these two former Confederates to bring action against Phillips, but Vaughn's suit asked for and received an attachment to be levied on the Hawkins County property of Phillips, who, by this time, according to census information, resided in Arkansas. On April 11, 1866, the sheriff of Hawkins County reported back to the Rogersville Circuit Court regarding the attachment, stating the one-hundred-acre tract of land belonging to Phillips situated in the Third Civil District or War Gap area of Hawkins County had been located and levied.

The other action against Phillips—a grand jury indictment apparently from the same Hawkins County one that delivered the Byrd murder indictment—accused Phillips of treason. According to this indictment, John Phillips was living at the time in Sabner County, Tennessee.[184] But strangely, no history of a Sabner County could be located. It's suspected that the court clerk misspelled or incorrectly recorded this critical information. The name Sabner may be a poor spelling of Sumner, an upper-middle Tennessee county by the same name formed in 1786, with Gallatin as the county seat. Obviously, if Sumner is correct, it appears to have been only a temporary residence for Phillips before moving on to Arkansas.

The indictment went on to describe Phillips on March 11, 1862,

> *intending to stir, to move, and excite insurrection, rebellion, and war against the state of Tennessee and in order to fulfill and bring to effect the said traitorous imaginations and indignations of him the said John Phillips. He the said John Phillips on the day and year foresaid, with force and arms in the County and State aforesaid, with a great multitude of persons, whose names to the Jurors aforesaid are unknown, to-wit: Thirty persons and upwards, armed and arrayed in a warlike manner, that is to say with*

guns, pistols, swords, and other warlike weapons, as well as offensive and defensive, did falsely and traitorously join and assemble themselves together against the State of Tennessee, and then and there with force and arms, did falsely and traitorously, and in a hostile and warlike manner arrayed and dispose themselves against the State of Tennessee.

The indictment listed three separate charges for indicting Phillips:

furnishing or supplying wheat, bacon and other provisions to the sum of $1000 dollars …apparently to those assembled;

By joining to the armies to the Confederate states…and enlisting men in its service;

And by holding a commission in the rebel army…… and other wrongs (unnamed) and injuries.

Despite a subsequent summons being issued by the court for John Phillips, it appears—and maybe for obvious reasons—Hawkins authorities declined to act upon or pursue further this particular grand jury indictment. Like similar court actions during the immediate post–Civil War era, many actions were brought by Unionists for treason and even murder, but few made it through the courts.

CHAPTER 11

Search for Justice Continues

The only justice obtained by the Byrd family from the death of Captain William K. Byrd appears to have come from court action noted earlier, initiated in Hawkins County Circuit Court beginning in the summer of 1865 and ending around 1878. As mentioned, this action accused the defendants of "trespass," a civil violation and not murder, as alleged in the October 1865 grand jury indictment. William's son, Andrew J. Byrd, the administrator of his father's estate, was the plaintiff in this suit.

In the trespass trial, the circuit court on February 1, 1866, "severally rendered judgments against…and in favor of the plaintiff" against five men: William S. Creed, John Wolf, Abijah Anderson, George Alexander and James Sevier. Of the five, Wolf, Creed and Sevier never made the 1865 grand jury murder indictment. In fact, the trespass action surprisingly included several women, who also failed to make the murder indictment. That same day, after rendering its judgments, the court issued new summonses for Eaton Pullen of Jefferson County, James Grantham and James Long of Grainger County and William K. Mays and Eli A. Cox of Hawkins County and dismissed the suit against fourteen other men for reasons unknown. Afterward, the court gave permission to the fourteen defendants to make recovery of their legal costs from the estate of William K. Byrd.[185] The court also noted several ancillary attachments (a legal device used to seize and hold property until resolution of a claim) as being returned unlevied for the following men: George W. Moore, Swimsfield Anderson, John W. Phillips, William S. Rose, Samuel McCullough, David McCoy, David McCullough,

Hiram Miles, Barnet Cantwell, Hiram Tucker, Clinton Tucker and the heirs of Swimpfield Anderson. With this unsuccessful effort to attach property, Andrew J. Byrd asked the court via attorney for permission, which was granted, for issuance of new judicial attachments on defendant property situated in several outlying counties.

A few months later, on June 6, 1866, on motion by the plaintiff, the court issued a writ requiring the following individuals to appear and show cause on why the action brought by Andrew J. Byrd against them should not be continued or revived: Abjah Ezekiel, George Anderson, Moses Anderson, James Martin and wife Mary, John Wilson and wife Martha, William Heord and wife Mary and Andrew J. Wilson and wife Ann, along with Sarah Hartley, Martha Hartley, George Hartley, and Swimpfield A. Hartley.[186]

Then, a year later, on June 4, 1867, Andrew dismissed his suit against Eli A. Cox and Eaton Pullen. Later in the fall term of the Hawkins Circuit Court, on September 30, 1867, the remaining defendants entered a new motion, asking for dismissal of the suit against them, noting the following six reasons:[187]

1. Because a "chasm or breakdown in the proceedings" between September 1865 and the following February 1866 term created a "discontinuance in the process."

2. Due to improper handling of the legal process involving several defendants.

3. Due to several defendants, such as George W. Moore and others as noted, not being brought into court.

4. The absence of several defendants, such as John D. Riley, James Long, Hiram Tucker, James Grantham, William K. Mayes and Clinton Tucker from the various processes. Their names were merely written with many others on pieces of paper pasted to the processes, thus negating or leaving the writ and bond with no application.

5. The plaintiff, or Byrd, had declared against a portion of the parties without disposing of the others.

6. The defendants John D. Riley, James Long, James Grantham, William K. Mayes, Hiram Tucker and Clinton Tucker moved to dismiss the suit because there was no prosecution or attachment bond as to them. They also moved to suppress judicial attachments because of insufficient due process.

The court apparently took the above motion under advisement, not making any immediate ruling. But a year later, in the fall of 1868, the parties returned to court on October 8, with the defendant's motion still outstanding from the previous September 1867. In this latest session, the court indicated the motion from September 1867 remained under review regarding the effect of the ancillary and judicial attachments, along with the defense's request for dismissal of the case. In addition, the plaintiff introduced Moses Anderson as the administrator for Swimpfield Anderson, who testified as to Swimpfield's death in October 1865—knowledge of which failed to elicit any objection from either party. In regard to Anderson's death, the court ruled "there was no discontinuance of the suit," and that the motion made at the September term "was overruled so far as it rested upon that ground."

This resulted in Byrd dismissing his suit against Swimpfield Anderson but obtaining judgment on Moses Anderson, Swimpfield's administrator. This surprising action, due apparently to Moses having failed to make proper appearance in court after "being routinely called," undoubtedly left him in disfavor with the court.[188] In addition, Byrd's legal counselor made another motion to issue a second summons for H.G. Wax, John D. Riley, George Moore, John Phillips, William S. Rose, Barnet Cantwell, Hiram Mills, David McCoy, Samuel McCullough, William K. Mayes, Hiram Tucker and Clinton Tucker. As a result of this motion, Byrd received permission from the court to "take leave" to mend and execute a new bond against the above-named defendants.

This session concluded with Byrd's attorney introducing Elias Beal, until recently the sheriff of Hawkins County, who stated that he had made a diligent search for all of the defendants listed in the original summonses. The plaintiff then asked that Beal be allowed to "modify his returns" or summonses of those defendants to reflect "them not being located or served." The court immediately responded by questioning the legality "of permitting a sheriff, "not now in office," to make changes or amendments to summonses. Former sheriff Beal had left office on March 4, 1868. As a result, the court failed to rule but decided to continue this additional question under advisement. The defendants concluded this session by objecting to the matters testified by Beal and Moses Anderson and offered a bill of exceptions to the court for inclusion in the court record. On Thursday, January 28, 1869, the defendants, by attorney, came back into court with motions seeking to strike the declaration and the cause from the court docket, effectively killing the action against them. The court overruled both motions, giving the defendants until the next term of the court to plead.[189]

In September 1869, this legal boxing match resumed, this time with the court giving opinions on two of three critical points taken under advisement earlier; the two involved the "status of the summons and ancillary attachments, and the plaintiff's request to allow former Sheriff Beal to modify his returns." On the first opinion, the court ruled in the defendants' favor, stating they could not be brought into court by the summonses and ancillary attachment described in the motion, without previous personal service of a summons prior to the other proceedings. On the second point, the court ruled again for the defendants, stating that ex-sheriff Elias Beal could not be permitted to modify his returns (or summonses) after leaving office, thereby showing them as "not found in the County." This latter ruling, if it had gone the other way, would likely have resulted "in the plaintiff maintaining his process against those defendants."[190]

The result of those opinions obviously dealt a very serious blow to the Byrd family's legal attempts to obtain justice and restitution for their father's death. These opinions resulted in the suit being dismissed against George Moore, John Phillips, William S. Rose, David McCoy, David McCullough, William K. Mayes, Hiram Tucker and Clinton Tucker. All of the men were permitted to recover their personal cost of the suit from assets of the plaintiff and estate of William K. Byrd. But probably more disappointing to the Byrds than any expense caused by the dismissals was the psychological and emotional impact of John W. Phillips, the former Rebel captain, being allowed to escape from this legal action. Next to Joseph B. Heiskell, Captain John W. Phillips may have been the second most powerful man connected with the Byrd raid.

With these dismissals and especially Phillips's, the Byrd family surely recalled the various testimonies given in Hancock County Chancery Court connecting Phillips and his men to the raid. The powerful testimony seemingly offered undeniable proof of Phillips and his raiding party's involvement and possible criminal action. Incriminating testimony showed Phillips not only present at the raid but also giving a command releasing the wounded Byrd to a fellow officer for the purpose of execution. Particularly notable were testimonies by Samuel Eidson and Nelson G. Seal, with Eidson recounting Phillips's own words admitting his personal involvement in the raid and of releasing the wounded Captain Byrd to his lieutenant.

Likewise, the testimony of Nelson Seal, a District Six resident of Hancock County, substantiated once and for all Phillips's involvement and that of other members of Company E, Forty-third Tennessee Infantry in the Byrd raid. If only these same testimonies had been given in a criminal court, as opposed to a civil proceeding, it might have been enough to convict Phillips and some of his men. In the end, it is conceivable the Byrd family may have deemed Phillips far more responsible for their father's death than even

Joseph B. Heiskell, Joseph Huffmaster, Larkin Eidson or possibly John Gray Bynum. As a result of the above judgment, Andrew J. Byrd, by his attorney, filed a bill of exception to the judgment and received permission to file a writ of error to the next term of the state Supreme Court in Knoxville, set to open the second Monday in September. The court further ruled, but this time in Byrd's favor, that several other defendants not previously dismissed had been properly brought into court, and the process kept up to date.[191]

The remaining defendants on Byrd's trespass suit included: Moses Anderson (administrator of Swimpfield Anderson), Henry Wax, Barnett Cantwell, John D. Riley, Hiram Mills and Samuel F. McCullough. The court also permitted a new declaration to be filed by the plaintiff against these men. After the above rulings, both sides immediately offered bills of exception to the court; the plaintiff complained about the suit being restricted to the men named above, and the defendants objected to the court allowing the suit to be continued. Both exceptions were added to the official court record. This trial session in September 1869 concluded with the court ordering the declaration filed in the September term of 1867 to be removed from the file, saying it had been prematurely filed. But the court allowed the same declaration to be left or made part of the Supreme Court record. This particular action resulted in the plaintiff filing yet another bill of exception, disagreeing with the removal of the declaration from the record.

After the dismissal of John W. Phillips, the court case of Andrew J. Byrd against the various persons believed to be connected with the Byrd raid dragged on for nine more years, but losing Phillips probably signaled the beginning of the end for the Byrd family's search for justice. After the fall of 1869, Andrew's legal struggle ground almost to a halt, with the case being continued through several terms of the court with little or no apparent activity by either party. Also, any Supreme Court proceedings or decisions evolving from this case, relating to the several writs of error and other exceptions filed by the parties, are unknown. After 1869, the only significant action apparently occurred in Hawkins County Circuit Court on September 26, 1871, from an affidavit submitted by defendant Barnett Cantwell.[192] This affidavit resulted in the court asking Byrd to give additional or sufficient security on his bond or justify his present security by the next term of the court, or his attachment against Cantwell would be dismissed.

After September 1871, the case slowed even further, with it being continued through several terms until September 28, 1876, when the "death of Andrew J. Byrd is suggested" by the court.[193] It's not known why the court thought Byrd had died, especially when it's known that Andrew J. Byrd lived apparently through the 1880 census. But on October 4, 1877, the court ordered Byrd to "come and prosecute his suit by the second day of the next term" or face dismissal of his suit. At the succeeding term, on February 2, 1878, the plaintiff, or Andrew J. Byrd, failed to make appearance to prosecute his suit as ordered by the court.[194] This failure resulted in the suit being dismissed by the court, and the remaining defendants were allowed to recover their cost of the suit from the prosecution bond, previously posted by Byrd and his nephew, James A. Bird, believed to be James A. "Dick" Byrd. This final action apparently ended the long and difficult thirteen-year effort by the Byrd family to obtain justice and restitution for the death of their father and grandfather, Captain William K. Byrd. No further court action is found to have occurred after this date.

CHAPTER 12

Hancock-Hawkins Counties: A Bridge Burning Connection?

T here is some evidence that exists to suggest Loyalists in Hancock and Hawkins Counties were early partners, or confidants, in Carter's plan to disable railroads in east Tennessee. In fact, several factors, now known regarding the activities of local Hancock and Hawkins Unionists in 1861 seem to suggest this possibility.

To begin with, William Blount Carter, chief planner and leader of the bridge burners, was a former resident of Hawkins County before the war, having been a Presbyterian minister and church pastor in the town of Rogersville until poor health forced him to resign. As a natural consequence of Carter's residency and resulting familiarly of the surrounding area, it's natural to assume Carter still possessed a core group of former friends and family living nearby, able and willing to assist in formulating and even participating in his bridge burning plot. In the wake and urgency of planning the bridge attacks, Carter may have turned to his old Hawkins County acquaintances and nearby Hancock County Loyalists for support and recruitment in the covert operation.

Another important factor supporting a possible link between Hawkins and Hancock County Unionists and the bridge burners relates to Captain David Fry of Company F, Second Tennessee Infantry Regiment. Captain Fry, a well-known and influential Unionist from Greene County, Tennessee, was one of two Union officers, along with William Cross of Scott County, assigned by the military to accompany Carter in carrying out the November 8 bridge attacks.[195] Fry had left east Tennessee earlier in the summer of 1861 for Kentucky, with his ultimate destination being Camp Dick Robinson, the Union military recruiting and training camp. Receiving a captain's commission, Fry organized F Company in late September 1861 and mustered it into the Second Tennessee Regiment at Camp Wild Cat on October 26, 1861, according to official records.

In filling the ranks of F Company, Fry recruited several men from Hawkins and Hancock Counties, all identified residents who would serve initially under Fry during that critical fall of 1861. Of the Hancock and Hawkins men serving under Fry, they included none other than James Anderson Bird— eldest son of Captain William K. Byrd—a strong, ardent Union supporter and recruiter who served in F Company as a second lieutenant until he was accidentally wounded by a fellow officer about November 30, 1861, barely three weeks after the bridge burnings. Along with Lieutenant Bird, his two young sons, William K. and John S. Byrd, and brother-in-law Private William Kelly appear to have served in Fry's company as well.

In addition to Byrd family members, other Hawkins and Hancock men serving in Fry's F Company included Levi Viles, a close friend and personal recruit of Lieutenant Bird, and Private Thomas Gibson, a next-door neighbor of Hancock County Unionist leader Joel Jarvis and fellow Loyalist John Wiatt (Wyatt?). Still other Hancock men serving in Fry's company included James O. Berry; Andrew J. Britt (Byrd?), possible brother of James A. Bird; P.L Berry; Private Isaac Goins; and Martin Merrell (Murrell?), who, according to records, may have served in I Company of the Second Infantry Regiment as well as Fry's F Company. Also, Private Isaac Goins appears to have served with F Company from October 1861 to December 1862.

Along with the others, a rather high-profile Hancock County Unionist by the name of Charles Barton also served in Fry's company; he had been the local representative to the Unionist Greeneville convention the previous summer. Besides his service with F Company, Barton appears to have also served in G Company, a unit commanded by Abraham H. Cross and Evan B. Jones. Barton was arrested along with fellow Hancock resident and Union militia captain Joel Jarvis back in September 1861 and brought before the East Tennessee Confederate District Court in Knoxville. During the court session, authorities brought charges accusing both men "of going to Kentucky earlier that summer and conspiring with Andrew Johnson." This was about the same time that the local Hancock County sheriff confided in Confederate general Flex Zollicoffer of an imminent large-scale Unionist attack on the area with "the intentions of destroying the railroad and halting transportation on the East Tennessee and Virginia line."

Hancock-Hawkins Counties: A Bridge Burning Connection?

This apparent belief by the Hancock sheriff, almost three or four months before the November 8 bridge attacks, sounded eerily similar to Carter's plan and the ultimate actions by Unionists. Moreover, the east Tennessee and Virginia line did in fact have two bridges destroyed during the attacks, one over the Holston at Union Depot and the other at Lick Creek near Greeneville, making the Hancock sheriff's earlier warning seem not only prophetic but having factual basis as well. The combination of those summer events in Hancock County and information of a possible plot against the railroads being uncovered would seem to suggest local knowledge and possible awareness on the part of Hancock and Hawkins Unionists to Carter's plans if not downright participation in formulating and carrying out the attacks.

William B. Carter, along with Captain David Fry and possibly William Cross, returned to Tennessee in late October for the purpose of coordinating the bridge attacks. It's not known if anyone else, including the Hawkins or Hancock men recruited by Fry, traveled with Carter's group on their return trip to east Tennessee. Although by this time, Fry had long since demonstrated a reputation for mobilizing and recruiting Union men, a talent not unnoticed by Carter—a talent Fry would put to good use once onsite in east Tennessee. Furthermore, Fry and Cross had intimate knowledge of their respective areas of operation, not to mention the existence of two targeted bridges in each man's home area, which was, no doubt, another critical reason for Carter selecting both men. Also, Oliver Temple, in his book *East Tennessee and the Civil War*, referred to David Fry, like many other Unionists, as a "brave, daring man, just suited for such an undertaking" as burning bridges.

In planning the attacks, Carter, Fry and Cross more or less divided up the targeted bridges, resulting in each man taking responsibility for planning their attacks and recruiting the necessary local leaders and volunteers. Fry's focus included the Lick Creek Bridge located in Greene County, while Cross is believed to have overseen the attack on the Loudon Bridge in Loudon County. Another interesting fact regarding Captain Fry's F Company has to do with Fry's actions on the night of the Lick Creek Bridge attack on November 8, 1861. Just prior to the attack, Fry swore in several of the bridge burners to his F Company; those men included Jacob Harmon Jr.; Henry Harmon, son of Jacob; Christopher A. Haun; Henry Fry; and Jacob M. Hinshaw. Sadly, four of these men, including the Harmons, Fry and Haun would be executed for their involvement in the attack.

Once the bridge burnings were over, Fry would reorganize and continue giving Confederates trouble by tearing up railroad tracks and telegraph lines between Chattanooga, Tennessee, and Marietta, Georgia, not to mention stealing two locomotives, before taking refuge in the Unionist stronghold of the Shelton Laurel area of Madison County, North Carolina. Using Shelton Laurel as home base, Fry, with his small band of guerrillas, would make numerous forays during the winter of 1862 against Rebels in east Tennessee and western North Carolina. But by April 1862, Confederates had long since tired of the depredations caused by Fry's band and began closing in on Shelton Laurel. Thus, under increasing pressure from Rebels, Fry attempted to lead his men to safety in Kentucky, only to be captured and sent off to prison in Atlanta. Soon after his imprisonment, the Rebels sentenced Fry to hang for his crimes against the Confederacy; but remaining sly as ever, Fry managed to escape from prison, reaching Kentucky. Having avoided the hangman's noose, Fry would later join another ill-fated mission, the Andrews Railroad Raid.

The story of Captain David Fry, in some respects, was similar to another Civil War guerrilla raider and hell raiser, but on the Confederate side—the notorious William Clark Quantrill of Missouri. Like Captain David Fry, Quantrill is believed to have been given a captain's commission early on in the Confederate army. Also, both men were probably the dashing, free-spirited hero to their supporters, but Quantrill, unlike Fry, was known for his ruthless and bloodthirsty acts against pro-Union and antislavery forces, especially in Kansas. In fact, during an 1863 raid on Lawrence, Kansas, Quantrill's guerrilla force of about 450 men rounded up and killed 183 men (including boys as young as fourteen) within hours. This event became infamously known as the Lawrence Massacre. As far as Fry and his guerrilla acts, there is nothing known regarding Fry's record that smacks or even approaches the Lawrence Massacre, although one author does suggest Fry brutalized captured guards during the Lick Creek Bridge burning on the night of November 8, 1861 by beating them up "just for the fun of it." This physical act, if it occurred, should not be minimized; but if it did, it seems extremely minor compared to the killing and mayhem inflicted by Quantrill and his men.

So how much did Charles Barton, Joel Jarvis, Second Lieutenant James A. Bird, Captain William K. Byrd and the other Hancock and Hawkins Loyalists really know regarding Carter's plan? Also, did any of these same men volunteer and participate with Fry, not just in the Lick Creek

Bridge and other attacks but in later guerrilla raids led by Fry? It's strongly suspected, and only reasonable to assume, that at least some of these men were influenced by Fry to take part or participate in the bridge burnings and later guerrilla raids. On second thought, can one conclude that Carter and Fry were prevented from fully using local Hawkins and Hancock men not only in the bridge attacks but later raids due to the arrest, injury and death later that fall by some of those counties' Unionist leaders? Until further information comes to light, one can only speculate.

CHAPTER 13

Was It Conspiracy and Murder or a Military Engagement?

W as the strike against Captain William K. Byrd and his militia in December 1861 a planned military action, conceived and guided by the high command of a young and still developing Confederate army? Or was it a conspiracy locally conceived and implemented by what some called a "marauding gang" of Confederate sympathizers or guerrillas, operating independently and apart from the regular Confederate army? Also, what role, if any, did Rogersville resident and Confederate congressman Joseph Brown Heiskell play in the raid? Was Heiskell present, as Parson Brownlow claimed, that December day on the north side of Clinch Mountain? Or was his connection more distant and removed, with personal involvement being nonexistent or no greater than providing political influence and support for the attack on Byrd's militia? In addition, how much knowledge of the raid, especially prior to the event, did Heiskell and the higher Confederate government possess? These questions and others evolving from the raid may never be fully answered, but surviving fragments of information found so far appear to offer at least some plausible answers or conclusions to these nagging questions.

Evidence so far appears to support the belief that the raid resulted from a locally conceived plot, with the action unknown by higher Confederate military authorities. One of the things supplementing this notion is the fact that the men of E Company would not be fully mustered into the regular Confederate army and Forty-third Regiment at Knoxville until a week or more after the raid. Also significant, E Company formed just the month before at Rogersville on November 5 and likely remained heavily concentrated with original recruits from the surrounding area, with the same recruits suspected of harboring strong feelings against Byrd and other Unionists active in the area since late spring. It's believed the bridge burnings the previous month only intensified those ill feelings and conveniently provided justification they probably sought to silence Byrd and his troublesome home guard once and for all. It's felt that the Rebels literally "seized the moment" ahead of full muster "to take Byrd out" and resolve what may have been viewed as "strictly a local problem"—a local problem some may have thought better dealt with while free of "regimental command interference and requirements" to explain and justify questionable actions to higher authorities.

No lasting record of the raid can be found in the history of the Forty-third Infantry, further supporting the local conspiracy theory and providing credence that Captain John W. Phillips's men and other sympathizers operated apart and separate from the higher Confederate command. On the other hand, in similar situations, especially later in the war, Confederate authorities had a tendency, including those as high as the secretary of war, to try and sweep these types of raids or guerrilla actions under the carpet. One of the most notable examples—one referred to previously—involved a similar "unionist raiding episode" carried out in January 1863 in Madison County, North Carolina, by members of the Sixty-fourth North Carolina Regiment, CSA. Known as the Shelton Laurel Massacre, it involved thirteen Unionist prisoners, ranging in age from thirteen to fifty-nine, who Confederates rounded up and shot to death.[196] In its aftermath and despite overwhelming evidence against the two accused Confederate officers, both men managed to go free. An army investigation initiated by the Confederate secretary of war less than two months after the Shelton Laurel killings failed miserably, resulting in a report containing a "jumble of contradiction and evasion." In fact, the report took so long to complete that one of the accused squirmed his way to freedom. Apparently, the army performed the investigation in such a way as to do "just enough to give the illusion of activity, but not enough…to stain the Confederate army with the blood of Shelton Laurel."

As far as the Byrd raid, no evidence has been uncovered so far to indicate its aftermath reached the same high levels of Confederate military and government as did the Shelton Laurel raid. The situation and political climate differed considerably in December 1861 versus January 1863. It's felt that the Byrd raid, coming so soon after the bridge burnings, and if

Was It Conspiracy and Murder or a Military Engagement?

A monument to Shelton Laurel Massacre was placed near the graves of the thirteen victims in David Shelton Cemetery, Marshall, North Carolina. *Courtesy of the author's collection.*

known by higher Confederate authorities in Knoxville or Richmond, might have deemed it necessary and expedient in view of the perceived Unionist threat prevailing at the time. Unionist activities on the North side of Clinch, according to various commentaries, had been escalating since late spring or early summer of 1861, and until the bridge burnings, those activities may have been viewed mostly as a nuisance or minor irritation by Confederate authorities. But after November 8 and the hysteria that followed, Byrd and his militia activities surely took on greater significance. From a purely local level, the elimination of Byrd, a sixty-something-year-old captain, and the likely fragile and untrained home guard, consisting probably of older men and boys barely into their teens, might have offered an attractive target for a newly formed military unit like E Company, no doubt eager to prove its worth in the expanding conflict.

Furthermore, beyond Captain John W. Phillips, the information uncovered so far fails to link any of the senior officers of the Forty-third to the Byrd raid. Neither of the regimental field officers at the time, Colonel James W. Gillespie or Lieutenant Colonel David M. Key, are mentioned in any of the postwar Hawkins County indictments or three surviving commentaries detailing the raid and death of Byrd. Although, as previously noted, Colonel Key led a similar expedition by the Forty-third Regiment against the Unionist stronghold of Sheldon Laurel in April 1862, barely five months after the Byrd raid, it's unknown if E Company participated in that expedition[197]

With the above being said, the ultimate responsibility and control for the Byrd raid and its execution seems to fall squarely on the shoulders of Captain John W. Phillips and his immediate command. Paramount is the damning and incriminating testimony from the Hancock County Chancery Court proceedings offered after the war by several Hancock County residents, including two of Byrd's own sons, which provided very creditable evidence to the guilt of Captain John W. Phillips and several under his command.

Another critical question regarding the raid relates to Confederate congressman Joseph Brown Heiskell and his whereabouts that December day in 1861. Did Heiskell go along with the raiding party as William G. "Parson" Brownlow claimed? Parson, from his Knoxville newspaper, provided strong and scathing accusations regarding Heiskell's involvement in the raid, even charging Heiskell of "tying up, and shooting…poor old Bird full of bullet holes," but Parson failed to fully expand on his accusations with more creditable evidence. In fact, none of the other commentaries or court records found so far come close to corroborating Parson's version. Unfortunately, Parson's comments on the Byrd raid, while not discounted totally, seem more akin to one of Brownlow's typical and sometimes exaggerated verbal tirades—a bitter reflection of his known dislike and hatred of any dedicated Rebel, especially one of Joseph Heiskell's statue.

On the other hand, Parson's son, John Bell Brownlow, a member of Gillem's Union command when they captured Heiskell had his own comments regarding the congressman. Like his father, John Bell brought strong accusations against Heiskell, stating he had been an accomplice "to the atrocious murder of several Union citizens." John Bell further stated that Heiskell "had accompanied and encouraged a band of rebel bushwhackers and thieves who lacerated with whips the backs of the wives, sisters, and daughters of Union soldiers," prompting General Gillem to take special steps to prevent Union soldiers from taking Heiskell's life. Considering John Bell's Union army service in East Tennessee, he no doubt witnessed firsthand some of those Union atrocities, making his accusations against Heiskell seem more creditable than his father's.

In addition to John Bell's comments, Heiskell, at the time of the Byrd raid, had only recently been elected as Confederate congressman for District One, the result

Colonel John Bell Brownlow, like his father, expressed strong accusations regarding Joseph Heiskell and his apparent covert activities in east Tennessee. *Courtesy of Tennessee State Library and Archives.*

of elections in early November 1861. As congressman-elect, he wouldn't assume his new duties until the First Confederate Congress convened in Richmond, Virginia, the following February 1862. During most of 1861 to early 1862, the Confederacy operated under a "provisional government" put in place in February 1861. Confederate provisional records fail to reflect any involvement by Heiskell with this early government. Thus, it doesn't appear Heiskell's new position or responsibilities in government would have kept him away from his Rogersville home and Hawkins County area during the first week in December 1861.

Another important consideration relates to Heiskell's general awareness and knowledge of Unionist activities during the late summer and fall of 1861. It's felt that Heiskell, by the time of the raid, possessed ample knowledge and awareness of Byrd and other Unionists operating near his home and District One congressional area, which consisted of Hawkins, Hancock, Greene, Carter, Washington, Sullivan, Johnson and Cocke Counties. Much of the awareness came from Heiskell's own work or recent practice, along with sixteen other lawyers, before the East Tennessee Confederate District Court in Knoxville the previous September. It was in this same court that several Unionists from Hawkins and Hancock Counties, including members of the Byrd family, endured trials on treason charges. Joseph Brown Heiskell, a prominent Rogersville resident, lawyer and rising secessionist, possessing extremist feelings against Unionist and possibly inflamed by the recent bridge burnings, no doubt had the political and personal motives "to see the Byrd problem eliminated as soon as possible."

Before continuing, it should be mentioned in Heiskell's defense, that two of the three known surviving commentaries on the Byrd raid failed to indicate Heiskell as a participant in the raiding party despite other information suggesting otherwise. Also, with Heiskell's recent election victory—barely a month before the raid and resulting in his elevated statue in the Confederate government—it would only seem logical that, if he were involved, more would have been said and documented by local Rogersville Unionist Crawford W. Hall and possibly others or more prominent east Tennessee unionists such as Oliver Temple. Eliza Fain, who documented the raid soon after the event in a diary entry on December 26, 1861, only mentioned four actual participants by name. Along with Captain Byrd, these include her son Ike Fain and Buck Huffmaster in the December 26 entry and Gus Fig (Teague) in a separate entry three months later. No other participates are named by Eliza. Furthermore, the Fain and Heiskell families, both prominent Rogersville families, were well acquainted and friends and had taken strong stands for the Southern cause almost from the beginning of the conflict. It seems reasonable to believe that if Heiskell had been along that day, Eliza surely would have mentioned it in her diary.

In another strange twist, this involving the court documents surrounding the Byrd raid, why did the plaintiff, Andrew J. Byrd, initially list Heiskell as a defendant on his trespass suit, and then suddenly dismiss him barely two months later? What prompted this dismissal? Was it political? Did Heiskell offer a known alibi as to his whereabouts the day of the raid? Or was it the opposite, that his exact whereabouts couldn't be substantiated?

Heiskell's dismissal from the trespass suit may have allowed Hawkins County authorities to focus their limited efforts and resources on bringing him to justice on the more serious crime of murder voted by the grand jury.

Still yet, another possible factor for Heiskell's dismissal from the trespass action and, to an even greater extent, the murder charge could have stemmed from authorities operating under the "assumption or expectation" of Heiskell receiving amnesty from the Federal government. If so, this thinking probably colored the various decisions made regarding Heiskell by Hawkins County authorities and Andrew J. Byrd's legal counselor.

It could even have played a role in the subsequent inability of Hawkins County authorities to make an arrest of Heiskell. So, while it is troubling to think, did Hawkins authorities assume Heiskell's amnesty as a foregone conclusion? If so, this could explain their failure to seek or continue prosecution of Heiskell on both the Byrd murder indictment and civil action. In regard to actual amnesty for Heiskell, a petition would be submitted on his behalf to the U.S. House of Representatives but not until five years after the war in 1870.

Lastly, can this failure to prosecute be explained from the perspective of the plaintiff? Did the plaintiff, Andrew J. Byrd, and the Byrd family conclude the "hill was just too big to climb" in getting a judgment against Heiskell? Byrd and his legal counsel probably realized that Heiskell still had, even after the war, many high-placed friends and political connections, not to mention greater finances than Byrd or the average poor Unionist. This fact was fully demonstrated when a Rogersville deputy made several unsuccessful attempts to arrest Heiskell in Memphis on the Byrd murder warrant, only to be prevented from doing so by either an obliging local judge or Federal marshal sympathetic to Heiskell.[198] Obviously without Heiskell in a local Rogersville jail, any legal actions against him by the Hawkins County Circuit Court would accomplish little if anything. Furthermore, regarding the financial aspects, the Byrds were farmers and preachers, no doubt barely making ends meet. They, like many others during this period, lived under severe circumstances caused by the war and probably lacked the necessary finances to support themselves, much less sustain a long or drawn out legal effort. Facing such stark realities, the Byrds may have become discouraged or disillusioned at mounting a legal attack on such a powerful man as Heiskell, thus justifying a heart-wrenching decision to drop or exclude him from the processes.

Considering yet another aspect, it doesn't appear the Byrd family's failure to achieve convictions in the legal fight against Heiskell and the others was due to a lack of competent legal counsel. According to Hawkins County Circuit Court records in May 1866, the legal counsel for Andrew J. Byrd consisted of attorneys Thomas A.R. Nelson and John Netherland, both noted Unionists who, after the war, participated in several cases similar to the Byrds. As late as January 1869, court records indicated Nelson was still working on the Byrd case. But beyond these few records, the full extent and duration of Nelson and Netherland's legal work on behalf of the Byrds is not fully known. In any event, it's strongly suspected that, due the thirteen-year length of the Byrd legal fight and Nelson's own death in 1873, several different attorneys were utilized, with Nelson and Netherland probably the most renowned of any possible group.

With the likes of Nelson, who began his legal practice in the 1830s in nearby Washington County, Tennessee, and Netherland, a well-known local Rogersville attorney, these two probably provided the Byrd family with their best hope for winning the court battle with former Confederates. Prior to the war, Nelson had served two terms as attorney general of the First Judicial Circuit, was elected to Congress in 1859 and then reelected in 1861 as a Unionist to the U.S. Congress, only to be captured by Confederates

John Netherland represented Hawkins County at the Unionist convention in Greeneville, Tennessee, in June 1861. *Courtesy of George E. Webb Jr., Rogersville, Tennessee.*

President Andrew Johnson fought with radical Republicans during much of his time in office over Reconstruction changes and polices. *Courtesy of Library of Congress.*

while trying to escape to Washington. Nelson also was a leading member at the Unionist conventions in 1861, and after the war, he was a member of the legal counsel who successfully defended President Andrew Johnson in his impeachment trial in 1868. Nelson later served as a judge in the state Supreme Court in 1870 before passing away in 1873.[199]

Born in Virginia in 1808, John Netherland served as a Tennessee legislator and U.S. senator during the 1830s while living in Kingsport and Franklin, Tennessee. Around 1837, he moved to Rogersville and soon after married Susan McKinney, the daughter of noted Rogersville attorney John A. McKinney, and Netherland's apparent law partner. Netherland would share an office in Rogersville until McKinney's death in 1845. Netherland later represented the Whig party, opposing Isham Harris unsuccessfully in the gubernatorial race of 1859. At the onset of the Civil War, Netherland served as one of the representatives from Hawkins County to the Unionist Greeneville convention in 1861.[200] Interestingly, both John Netherland and John A. McKinney's families are interwoven in marriage with the Heiskell family. Sarah, the daughter of John A. McKinney, was the first wife of Joseph Brown Heiskell, and John Netherland's daughter, Eliza Ayer, was the wife of Carrick Heiskell, Joseph's brother. How these two relationships influenced or created possible conflicts of interest regarding Netherland and Nelson's attempt to represent Andrew J. Byrd and family in the suit against Joseph Brown Heiskell and others, is unknown. The ultimate impact, if any, on the Byrd case probably remains forever a mystery and a point of speculation.[201]

In view of the foregoing information, it would seem logical and appropriate at this point to conclude that Joseph Brown Heiskell didn't participate in the raiding party on the North side of Clinch Mountain that December day in 1861. That is, if it were not for two significant pieces of incriminating information disclosed in two articles in the *Knoxville Register*, the first on November 19 and other on December 26, 1861, with the latter written by the *Register*'s editor and owner, Jacob A. Sperry, a strong secessionist and devoted supporter of the Southern cause. The November 19 article tells of Rebel citizens from Hawkins, Sullivan and Washington Counties, estimated at five hundred, gathering at Carter's Depot within days of the November 8 bridge burnings and forming a regiment. According to the article, the following regimental officers were elected: "Hon. Joseph B. Heiskell, member of C.S. Congress from the first congressional district...elected Colonel; Wm. L Rice, of Bristol, Lieut. Colonel; and J. G. Bynum [John Gray Bynum?] of Rogersville, Major." The article also noted this regiment of volunteers, along with Colonel Stovall's battalion numbering five hundred, and four artillery guns advancing soon after on Doe River Cove, where they found a deserted Unionist camp. Today, Doe River Cove is known as Hampton and lies about six miles south of Elizabethton, Tennessee. After the Doe River Cove action, the same article tells of Heiskell and Stovall's newly formed force arresting about thirty Unionist prisoners "in the knobs, each armed with gun, pistol and bowie knifes," with the prisoners being taken to Watuaga Bridge for anticipated transport to Knoxville to face the Confederate court.[202]

The second article of December 26 detailed an interview with Colonel Joseph B. Heiskell visiting in Knoxville that day, less than two weeks after the raid on Byrd's militia and a month after the Doe River Cove engagement in Carter County. The article stated Colonel Heiskell as "lately having rendered great service to the military authorities as commander of a volunteer force from Hawkins County, in the expedition against the insurgents of Carter County." While not directly mentioning or relating the Hancock raid in the article, Heiskell's own admission of having leadership in a local Hawkins County Confederate sympathizers group is very significant, not to mention highly incriminating—almost convicting—words, especially coming so soon after the Carter County action and Byrd raid.[203]

In addition, efforts by Heiskell's friends and associates to address him as either major or colonel were long standing, dating back before Tennessee's secession. The diary of Eliza Fain, a strong Southern supporter as previously noted and Rogersville area resident living near Heiskell, contains numerous references to Heiskell as a colonel. On the other hand, Heiskell, according to official Tennessee war records, never officially served in an organized Confederate military group. But surprisingly, there is evidence Heiskell was serving as a volunteer aide for Confederate colonel H.L. Giltner as late as November 1863, who commanded the Fourth Kentucky and Second Tennessee Cavalry Brigade, CSA. [204] This places Heiskell in a select group of men some historians refer to as "non-regimental enlisted men, who did not belong to any particular regiment, separate company or comparable unit, or special corps." Giltner was one of several Confederate commanders involved with the critical battles of Blue Springs in Greene County and Big Creek in Hawkins County during October and November 1863.

The only other recorded military or militia service by Heiskell was with a company of men and seven other companies organized in Rogersville in 1856. The companies were mustered following the murder of two local area residents by slaves and resulting fear of the town council of a possible slave insurrection. Any involvement Heiskell had in the 1856 company appears to have lasted only about a year before the companies were disbanded.[205] Even so, the above information regarding Heiskell and the Civil War clearly suggests a longstanding involvement, especially in late 1861 as a leader or senior leader in a local Hawkins County Confederate sympathizer group likely organized initially as a civilian or Confederate home guard that possibly evolved into E Company, Forty-third Tennessee Regiment, CSA, commanded by another Hawkins County resident, Captain John W. Phillips.

In light of the foregoing information, and Heiskell's admission in the Sperry article being paramount, the accusations noted earlier by Parson Brownlow and son John Bell seem more credible. With Heiskell's military involvement exposed by the *Register* articles, Parson's harsh accusations take on a different light and very well could have been closer to the actual truth than first perceived. In fact, both John Bell and his father may have had a more accurate knowledge of Heiskell's true involvement and therefore better understanding of his true Rebel character than credited by some historians. As a result, unless further information comes to light, it is believed Joseph Brown Heiskell was present during the raid on Byrd and held the top leadership position. In addition to his participation and leadership role, Heiskell, rather than Captain Phillips or John Gray Bynum, ultimately held final control over the decision regarding the execution of Captain Byrd. In the end, Captain Phillips's men, such as First Lieutenant Joseph Huffmaster and Second Lieutenant Larkin W. Eidson became "the doers of the deed," acting under orders from Heiskell and possibly Phillips.

If Confederate congressman Joseph Brown Heiskell led the raid, with help from Captain John W. Phillips's E Company and John Gray Bynum's civilian sympathizers, were they the ones who conceived it and possibly promoted it? Of the men personally involved, it's thought only three or four could have successfully conceived and promoted the raid against Byrd. Obviously, the leading candidates include Congressman Heiskell, Phillips, the thirty-four-year-old E Company commander, and maybe John Gray Bynum (who Crawford W. Hall adamantly claimed led the raid and local Confederate sympathizer group). Besides those three but less likely are Larkin W. Eidson, the thirty-one-year-old lieutenant who Andrew Byrd accused of leading the company that fateful day; Joseph Huffmaster, the twenty-three-year-old first lieutenant; and Sergeant Ike Fain, the eighteen-year-old "hot-headed" son of Eliza Fain. But the ages of Fain and Huffmaster, not to mention being outranked by Colonel Heiskell, Captain Phillips and Major Bynum, probably precluded all three from having any significant role in planning the raid. But all of these men, mostly local residents of Hawkins County and possessing strong secessionist feelings or coming from families that did, no doubt knew about Byrd and his family's Unionist activities. Needless to say, all became willing participants not lacking personal motivation to carry out the raid.

But who of the first three men could have conceived and possibly promoted this covert action, a person more powerful and influential than any of the others? Only one man possessed more power, greater than all the others combined; that man, of course, was Joseph Brown Heiskell, whose Hawkins County home today remains on the main street of Rogersville. Heiskell, with his recent election, resulting high government position and array of political connections, was soon to be—if not already—one of the most powerful men living in east Tennessee, certainty the most powerful in the Hawkins and Hancock area. Along with this increased stature and political position, Heiskell brought a certain level of extremism in his thinking regarding the handling of Unionist people. In fact, Oliver P. Temple described Heiskell as an extremist in his book, *East Tennessee and the Civil War*. More important, both Temple and Brownlow noted that the Confederate government at Richmond repeatedly looked to or sought out Heiskell's advice on policies relating to handling and disposition of Unionists.

The former home of Joseph B. Heiskell still stands on Main Street in Rogersville, Tennessee. *Courtesy of the author's collection.*

Consequently, after his election victory, the ultra secessionist could have possibly felt mounting pressure from local Confederate authorities and other Southern supporters around Hawkins and Hancock Counties "to handle the festering Unionist situation," with even himself probably angered and exasperated by Byrd's activities. Another harsh reality possibly pondered by Heiskell, and likewise contributing to his motivation to support a raid on Byrd, a reality more personal than the others, was the fact that the Unionist activities were simply too close to home, operating seemingly unimpeded only a few miles distance from his residence. In the end, Joseph B. Heiskell clearly had the position, ample reasons and motivation, both personally and politically, for seeing the Byrd situation swept away. In the end, Joseph Brown Heiskell not only had leadership of the raiding party but also was in the best position to have conceived and promoted it.

CHAPTER 14

Closing Reflections

While the court case by the Byrd family lasted for nearly thirteen years after the Civil War, key Confederates involved or accused of involvement in the raid seemingly returned to private life, with little or no apparent legal consequences being extracted as a result of their wartime activities. Joseph Brown Heiskell—the man who probably had more to do with promoting and spreading terror and fear among Union people of east Tennessee during the Civil War than any other—by 1870 once again entertained thoughts of a political career. Having survived the war, military prison, courtroom battles with Unionists like the Byrds and other hurdles, Heiskell set his sights on the last major roadblock standing in his way of full citizenship: he had to seek and obtain "relief from the political disabilities imposed by the 14th amendment of the U.S. Constitution." If this could be achieved, his citizenship would be fully restored and his political aspirations could take flight.

The Thirteenth, Fourteenth and Fifteenth Amendments are often referred to as the Civil War or Reconstruction Amendments, passed into law shortly after the war, with the Fourteenth being ratified on July 9, 1868. The problem faced by Joseph Heiskell had to do with paragraph three of the Fourteenth Amendment relating to persons holding political office. Briefly stated and regarding the United States, this section prevented any person who "shall have engaged in insurrection or rebellion against the same, or given aid or comfort to the enemies thereof" from holding any state or federal office. But the good news for Joseph Brown Heiskell was that this section made provisions for individuals to obtain relief from this political disability by filing a petition with Congress. The petition, if voted on and approved by a two-thirds vote of each house, would then remove the disability and allow the individual to hold political office.

On February 5, 1870, from Nashville, James S. Brown, a friend of Heiskell's and a member of the 1870 Tennessee constitutional convention, in a letter to the Honorable B.F Butler of Washington D.C., formally filed a petition on behalf of Joseph B. Heiskell with the U.S. House of Representatives, asking for Heiskell's relief from the political disabilities imposed by the Fourteenth Amendment.[206] Along with Heiskell, the letter also sought relief for three other former Confederates, Alexander W. Campbell, William D. Lawrence and James W. Porter, all three residing in west Tennessee at the time. The letter stated that all four had been "thoroughly identified with the South in the late war," and since getting their parole, they "had used their influence in the interest of peace and the enforcement of laws, (and) are gentleman of strict integrity and a high order of talent."

Referring to the 14th Amendment, Brown further stated he "understood that the 14th amendment was simply a precautionary and not a vindictive measure and that those affected by its operation were to be relieved as soon as they gave sufficient evidence of their friendliness to the government."

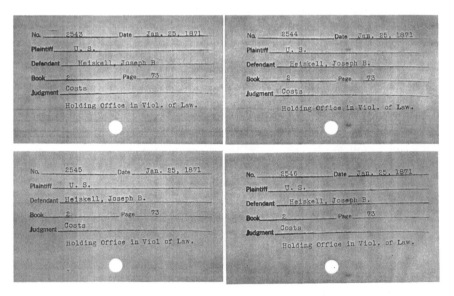

As late as January 1871, federal file cards indicate a suit was still pending against Joseph B. Heiskell for Fourteenth Amendment violations. *Courtesy of National Archives, Atlanta Ga.*

Brown concluded his commentary by giving several points of evidence why Heiskell and the others should be relieved of their disabilities, noting the "strict observance of their paroles, the love of and obedience to the laws, their disposition to protect all citizens without regard to race or color, and specifically their integrity, unquestioned by all who know them."

Surprisingly, Brown's letter to the U.S. Congress was either not successful or immediately acted upon by the House in granting relief for Joseph Brown Heiskell from the disabilities of the Fourteenth Amendment. According to federal court and newspaper articles of the day, Heiskell still remained on a list of cases pending for Fourteenth Amendment violations in the U.S. Circuit Court at Knoxville as late as December 1870 and February 1871. Furthermore, one source claimed Heiskell never received a pardon and ultimately became what many called an "unreconstructed rebel." Despite his personal situation, wartime service with the Confederate Congress and possible war crimes against Union people, Heiskell was called to public office beginning in 1870 as a member of the same state constitutional convention as his friend, James Brown.[207] Later that same year, while still under possible court action by the U.S. Circuit Court, Heiskell was appointed attorney general and reporter of the state of Tennessee, an office he held for eight years until 1878. Leaving office, Heiskell once again returned to his private law practice.

It should be noted that Joseph B. Heiskell's father, Frederick S. Heiskell, died at Rogersville on Thursday, November 30, 1882, age ninety-six, but neither son, Carrick W. nor Joseph B. attended their father's funeral.[208] This may not be surprising in view of the enormous animosity that surely continued to resonate as a result of Heiskell's wartime activities against local Union people still living in the Rogersville area. His brother, Carrick W. Heiskell, served with Company K, Nineteenth Tennessee Infantry, CSA, and died in Memphis on July 29, 1923. Joseph continued in his law practice in Memphis until his death on March 8, 1913, at the age of eighty-nine. Joseph was buried alongside his first wife, Sarah Ann McKinney, in the Evergreen section of the historic Elmwood cemetery in Memphis.[209] Along with Joseph and Sarah, several other Heiskell family members were buried in this same section.

As far as Captain John W. Phillips of E Company, Forty-third Tennessee Infantry, CSA, he relocated near the close of the war to Washington County, Arkansas, long before his dismissal from the Byrd court action in February 1869. According to census records, Phillips's son, also named John, was born in Arkansas in 1864.[210] Phillips continued to live in western Arkansas,

Above: Joseph B. Heiskell's gravestone is located in Elmwood Cemetery in Memphis, Tennessee. *Courtesy of the author's collection.*

Left: From left, the gravestones of first wife Sarah Ann McKinney and Joseph B. Heiskell in Elmwood Cemetery. *Courtesy of the author's collection.*

Right: The Heiskell family plot at Elmwood. *Courtesy of the author's collection.*

building a home in 1868 just west of the town of Springdale, where he and the family resided for many years. After moving to Arkansas, Phillips taught school for awhile but later opened a wagon factory in Springdale, which he conducted for a number of years. In his later years, around 1890, John closed the wagon factory and operated a mercantile and produce business, also in the Springdale area. The 1900 census listed John as a landlord, age seventy-five, a widower and living with his son, John, and Carrie Phillips's family in the Valley Township of Washington County.[211]

Captain John W. Phillips passed away in Springdale on July 18, 1907, with burial nearby in Bluff cemetery. With Phillips's death, the associated experiences and possible dark secrets from his service in the Confederate army likely died with him. "Uncle John," as friends and family affectionately called him in later years, had seemingly outlived any tarnished or unbecoming legacies caused by his war service. Phillips's obituary noted him as a man "held in high esteem by all who knew him," possessing "rugged honesty and sterling integrity, and his life…[being] above suspicion." On the day of Phillips's funeral, businesses closed out of respect in Springdale during the hour of his funeral.[212]

Isaac "Ike" Fain, released from jail in 1866 on a charge of "aiding and abetting" in the murder of Byrd, continued to live in the Rogersville area. By the following year, he was involved in a riot in Rogersville on July 23, 1867, and was arrested once again. This time, he was charged with robbery during the Civil War of three horses belonging to William Alvis. After his release on bond, Ike headed west like the Heiskell brothers, Phillips and many other local Confederate veterans.

But as late as October 7, 1867, Ike, according to court records, was still dealing with the Byrd murder indictment. On that date, in an affidavit to the Hawkins court, Ike "makes oath" requesting additional time to take certain depositions required from " John W. Phillips, Nicholay McCanty [*sic*], Joseph Huffmaster, Jr.," who all resided "beyond the limits of the state," so as to "prove…that he was not present and had nothing to do with the killing of the person, with which he is charged in the indictment; and [apparently claiming] at the time, he was several miles away, and was entirely ignorant of the transaction."[213] Ike's claim in this affidavit seems to contradict his own apparent comments made to his mother, Eliza, which she recorded in her diary soon after the fight, describing Ike and Buck Huffmaster narrowly escaping from the skirmish, and of Ike never feeling "so frightened in his life, with bullets flying by him and not being able to see."

Isaac "Ike" Fain and son Richard Rhea Fain, taken about 1890 in Chariton, Iowa. Like so many Rebels, Ike relocated to save his skin. *From* Sanctified Trial, The Diary of Eliza Rhea Anderson Fain, a Confederate Woman in East Tennessee, *with permission of the University of Tennessee Press, Knoxville.*

It should be noted, according to Eliza in another entry, Buck Huffmaster had been brought back wounded to Rogersville on December 5, two days ahead of the deadly fight with Byrd. So, if correct, was Buck's wound not severe enough to keep him from returning to duty near Sneedville prior to the fight and then participating with Ike in the fracas, like Eliza's December 26, 1861, entry leads us to believe, or did Buck's wound keep him from rejoining the raiding party, thus providing some creditable support for Ike's claim of being "several miles away" at the time of the raid? Of course, it's entirely possible the comments his mother related, placing Ike and Buck at the fight with Byrd, could have very well resulted when Buck was wounded, two or more days ahead of the actual raid and killing of Byrd. On the other hand, in a diary entry on December 6, the evening before the raid, Eliza placed sons Ike and Samuel away from home, "both across the mountains not many miles distant," thus leading us to conclude Ike definitely, and maybe Buck, were at the fight with Byrd and his militia.

Despite his involvement with the Byrd murder indictment and later charges of robbery, Ike never served any hard time for either offense. In 1868, Ike returned to Rogersville for his trial, but the case was never tried. Ike spent his later years living in Iowa. After his death in 1917, Ike was described as one of the most prominent citizens of Chariton, Iowa.[214]

As far as the Byrd family, Andrew J. Byrd, according to court records, lived into the late 1880s. No death date or burial location has been determined for him, but it's believed he was buried in northern Hawkins County in the Pumpkin Valley area. His brother, William Elliott "Ellie" Byrd appears to have outlived Andrew, passing away on January 18, 1898. Both men spent most of their adult life farming, with William having been a postmaster, Methodist and missionary Baptist preacher and justice of the peace at various times in his life. William also served for a time during the 1880s as elder and pastor of the Richardson Creek Baptist Church in northern Hawkins County.[215] William's war service or related activities included piloting or guiding Union men from Tennessee to Kentucky and lending his assistance after the war to his brother, Andrew J., in the legal fight on behalf of their deceased father. Also while not fully confirmed, one source indicated William having being captured while serving in 1864 with Company E, Eighth Tennessee Cavalry Regiment, USA. Still further information indicates William E. as being charged in Hawkins County Circuit Court in early 1866 with robbery and assessed a fine of $17.75, including court costs. While specific details of William's violation appear unavailable, it's felt that the action no doubt related to the Civil War, like so many others during this period.[216]

The youngest son, Levi Benjamin Bird, enlisted at the age of twenty-seven in Hancock County on September 23, 1863, and served with Company E, Eighth Tennessee Cavalry Regiment, USA, until mustered out on September 11, 1865, in Knoxville. During his service, Levi rose to the rank of first sergeant, and his pension papers described him as being an "honorable and upright citizen, with no vicious habits." It's not known if Levi served with his father's militia or was present the day his father was killed. But after his wartime service, Levi and his family continued to live in Tennessee until about 1873, thereafter moving to Green County, Iowa; later to Rooks County, Kansas; before settling about 1888 in King County, Seattle, Washington. In Seattle, Levi worked as a lumberyard superintendent for a number of years before retiring. He passed away in Seattle on November 1, 1924, at the age of eighty-eight. He is buried alongside his wife, Harriet J. (Babb) Bird in the Bothell IOF Cemetery.[217]

The eldest son, James Anderson Bird, probably suffered far more than any of his brothers as a result of the Civil War, excluding maybe Ephraim and, of course, their father. In fact, James, according to pension records, was wounded on or about November 30, 1861, about a week before his father died, while serving as a second lieutenant with Company F, Second Tennessee Infantry, USA. James and his regiment had been a major part of the bridge burning and invasion scheme, before William T. Sherman's "change of mind" order halted Generals Thomas and Carter at London, Kentucky. While at London and Camp Calvert, a fellow officer accidentally shot James in the face with a pistol. The wound was a very serious one, with the ball having entered just below the right eye near the nose, angling toward the left eye. Surgeons would struggle to remove the ball but failed to extract it. This wound affected his eyesight and gave him considerable pain and discomfort for the rest of his life. Unfortunately for James, an even greater demon waited just around the corner.

Soon after his father's death and sometime during James's recovery from his gunshot wound, his family fled to Kentucky after enduring much personal abuse and property destruction from continued Rebel harassment. After gaining a limited recovery from his gunshot wound, James returned to active duty, where soon after he made at least one or more forays into Hancock and Hawkins area during the winter of 1862–1863, recruiting men for Union service.[218] James was discharged due to disability on April 12, 1863. He spent the last two years of the war as a "sutter[219] for the 8th TN Cavalry Regiment USA." By war's end, James was feeling the symptoms of consumption and tending a mercantile store in Morristown, Tennessee. By 1868, as his pension papers related, his "consumption was far advanced and in its last stages," which left James and his family—now broken up—penniless, bankrupt and totally dependent on his daughter, Orlena, and her husband, S.J. Crouch, for all of their support.

Over the next three years, James's physical condition only worsened as his body was ravaged and decimated by disease, resulting in his death on December 2, 1871, in Russellville, Hamblen County, Tennessee.[220] His passing was a sad ending for a man who, with his father, William K. Byrd, may have contributed much to the support of Unionism in Hawkins and Hancock County area during those dark days of 1861. James's recruiting efforts and enthusiasm for Unionist speech making no doubt played a role in bringing Rebel vengeance down upon him and his family. But while it may be so, there appears to be no evidence of regret, at least in James's pension papers. James Anderson Bird was buried in the Old Russellville Community cemetery along Highway 11 East just one-fourth miles east of town on the south side and up the hill a short distance. James's grave lies in the southwest corner, or "older part of the cemetery," which sadly is terribly overgrown and dense with briars and weeds, making it nearly impossible to locate the grave until just recently.

Like sons Andrew J. and William E., no one has determined the burial site of Captain William K. Byrd. After his death, any burial by friends or family members was suspected of being done quickly, possibly under cover of darkness and in fear of their own lives for being captured or killed by the Confederate raiding party. It's felt that the person or persons performing

Above: A broken headstone lies adjacent to Bird's grave. *Courtesy of the author's collection.*

Below: The grave of Second Lieutenant James A. Bird, located in the Old Russellville Cemetery in Russellville, Tennessee. *Courtesy of the author's collection.*

The author kneeling at the foot of Bird's grave. *Courtesy of the author's collection.*

Captain Byrd's burial intentionally left his grave unmarked, possibly to protect against desecration by the same raiders who had taken his life.

As far as possible burial sites, William K. Byrd and his two sons may have been buried in the Byrd-Stapleton Cemetery, a burial plot located in an area known by some locals as Byrd Field, a high flat plain in northern Hawkins County lying just above Byrd Creek (Richardson Creek on some older maps), close to where it flows into Sweet Creek and not far from the intersection of Byrd Creek Road and Black Sheep Hollow Road. This cemetery contains over twenty-five unmarked graves, having only fieldstones as markers, along with about fifteen marked graves. It must be noted that this same cemetery, while recently known as the Byrd-Stapleton Cemetery, is also identified as the Tate Cemetery on the *Kyle's Ford Quadrangle, Tenn.-Va.* map dated 1947 (revised in 1969) and published by the U.S. Department of Interior Geological Survey.[221] Today, this cemetery, with recent cleanup and improvements in 2004, has four heavy cedar posts (telephone pole size) supporting the corners and fencing of the cemetery. A Byrd descendant, Mary J. (Byrd) Testerman Tate, daughter of William E. Byrd, was buried in the cemetery in a marked grave. Mary's second marriage was to a Robert Tate. It is rumored that the Tate family cared for the cemetery during the 1920s and '30s. In addition, there are two other unmarked graves that, for

Left: Arlie Drinnon, great-great-grandson of Captain Byrd, sits in the back row at left with son and the author in front, September 2001. Arlie was then living in Pumpkin Valley, northern Hawkins County. *Courtesy of the author's collection.*

Below: The Falls on Byrd Creek, located below Byrd-Stapleton Cemetery, just before Byrd merges into Sweet Creek near the Hawkins-Hancock County line. *Courtesy of the author's collection.*

Above: Byrd-Stapleton Cemetery gate view, looking northwest. This cemetery is situated on what some local residents call Byrd Field, which lies above Byrd Creek. *Courtesy of the author's collection.*

Right: Byrd-Stapleton Cemetery, looking west. *Courtesy of the author's collection.*

Below: Byrd-Stapleton Cemetery, looking south. *Courtesy of the author's collection.*

reasons unknown, lie just outside the main cemetery less than fifty yards south in a clump of trees near what the property owner said was an old "brick kilning area." It's possible one of those could be the grave of Captain William K. Byrd.

Another possible location for Captain Byrd's grave is about a mile away in a small hilltop cemetery located along Highway 66 in Hawkins County, known in county cemetery records as Byrd Cemetery. It is located just off the east (or right) side of the road, before it goes north over Pine Ridge toward Hancock County and the town of Sneedville. Several fieldstones outside of a small chain-link fence mark a number of graves in this cemetery. Buried just

Author standing in Byrd Cemetery on Highway 66, not far from Byrd-Stapleton Cemetery. The photo was taken in July 1998. *Courtesy of the author's collection.*

inside the chain-link fence is one of Andrew J. Byrd's grandsons, Walter Springfield Byrd, buried alongside wife Vera "Zura," both in marked graves. Walter, a World War I veteran, tragically died young a few days short of age thirty in 1926.

A fourth possible location for Captain William K. Byrd's grave, and the most likely resting place, lies in a cemetery on top or near the top of a ridge located just east and north of an intersection identified today as Black Sleep Hollow Road and Byrd Creek Road in far northern Hawkins County; it is only about half a mile from the Byrd-Stapleton or Tate Cemeteries previously noted. Considering the "highness and remoteness" of this location (and similar to that described in Eliza Fain's diary), this area may in fact be the site of the Byrd raid as well as the burial ground for Captain Byrd and other Unionists killed in the raid. This ridge-top cemetery can be located using the geological survey map identified as *Kyle's Ford Quadrangle*, by starting at the axis in the lower left-hand corner of the map and going approximately two thousand feet north and three thousand feet east. In other words, it's basically two thousand feet due east of the survey map intersection of Richardson's Creek Road (Byrd Creek Road) and the eastbound road, Black Sheep Hollow Road, while lying on the north side of the eastbound road. Interestingly, this cemetery today is above an old white house and barn situated or fronting Byrd Creek Road

Above: The front half of this home, located at Byrd Creek and Black Sheep Hollow Roads, Hawkins County, is thought to be the former home of William E. Byrd, according to local old-timers. *Courtesy of the author's collection.*

Below: The front of the William E. Byrd home. *Courtesy of the author's collection.*

at the same intersection, a house, according to old-timers, formerly owned by Captain Byrd's son, William Elliott "Ellie" Byrd. The property owner mentioned the existence of this cemetery several years ago. Unfortunately, as of the fall of 2010, the author has failed to gain permission to visit or inspect this cemetery and surrounding area.

In reflection, it must be acknowledged that the tragic events surrounding

Abraham Fulkerson. *Courtesy of Worsham, Old Nineteenth.*

the Byrd raid occurred all too frequently on both sides during the war and for some years after, and these killings were not, by no means, unique to Union people. The period after the Civil War, 1865–1869, is often called the Radical Republican period, and this period produced its own violent situations mostly against returning Confederate veterans and their families. In some ways, this postwar period mirrored the 1861–1862 "reign of the rebels," except after the war, the tables had been turned with radical Union men now in control and spreading their own brand of vengeance and terror upon former Confederates.

It was during this Radical Republican period that Union guerrilla groups perpetrated many atrocities, such as the one lead by the notorious William O. Sizemore. Beginning even before the war ended, and as Union troops mustered out of service, these acts of violence against Confederate veterans rose to epidemic proportions. During 1865 and early '66, Union veterans seemed to go on a rampage all over east Tennessee. One particular incident during the winter of 1865 involved a gang of Union bushwhackers who made a raid into Hawkins County, ransacking numerous homes and killing two Confederate sympathizers.[222] Needless to say, these lawless bands of Union sympathizers thought of themselves as self-appointed judges and juries, whose harsh treatment led many former Confederates to pack up and leave in order to protect their families and save themselves. Then there were a few individuals on both sides, like William K. Byrd, who stood their ground but, in the end, paid the ultimate sacrifice for their courage and beliefs.

It is also evident that Unionist attempts at restitution after the war only had partial success in the civil courts and even less success in the criminal courts at striking back at Rebels. Like the Byrd family, Unionists had little trouble obtaining indictments and even arresting the accused, but it was nearly impossible to obtain a conviction for a criminal offense, especially murder. In the end, many Confederates accused of various crimes and wrongs during the war sought relief from Unionist legal attacks by accepting President Andrew Johnson's amnesty proclamation of May 29, 1865, with the goal being the quick restoration of Southern states to the Union. Once an individual obtained presidential clemency, it meant the restoration of civil and property rights, but more importantly, it provided an escape from prosecution in the state civil and criminal courts as well.[223] For others who failed to qualify for Johnson's amnesty proclamation, being excluded by one of the fourteen exceptions, they could apply for "special pardon" from the president or Justice Department. Records indicate that 652 Tennesseans took this avenue, with about two-thirds of those requests coming from east Tennessee.[224]

In closing, the memorable words of Abraham Fulkerson are recalled regarding the Civil War. Fulkerson, a Confederate officer who served with both the Nineteenth and Sixty-third Tennessee Infantry Regiments, graduated from Virginia Military Institute. Wounded at Shiloh, Fulkerson later led the Sixty-third into battle at Chickamauga. He went on to serve in the U.S. House of Representatives. He gave a touching summary of the Civil War with the following words, written several years after its conclusion.

He had this to say:

> *The demons of war took possession of innocent and quiet homes, and reveled there until long after peace had been restored elsewhere. And yet, while there is much to deplore in the animosities engendered and the excesses perpetrated in this fratricidal war, we have reason to be proud of the courage and manhood exhibited by the citizen soldiers who went forth and confronted death at each other's hands, for what they conceived to be right. The descendents of the men who turned the tide of war at King's Mountain, New Orleans and Buena Vista should not be enemies of each other. Let us beat our swords into plowshares, and our spears into pruning hooks, and learn war no more; or, if we must fight, let it be with a common foe, shoulder to shoulder, in all time to come.[225]*

Captain William K. Byrd, a Union man from Hawkins County, Tennessee, was said to be a bold, daring and fearless man who some called a Lincolnite.

APPENDIX A

William K. Byrd Murder Indictment

Indictment

The State
vs
.... Phillips, Larkin
..doon d al

Murder

William E. Byrd & James
A Byrd — Prosentors

Summons for the State
William Sizemore
Brokeley D. Trent
Lucinda Burton
George W. Huntsman
Nancy Curry
James Davis
John B. Proffitt   186
E. Leivary   186
David Lovens
Fredrick Brewer

James Britton
X   A S

State of Tennessee) Circuit Court
Hawkins County   ) October Term 1865
                              The Grand Jurors for the
State being duly summoned elected empanneled
sworn and charged to inquire for the body of the
county aforesaid upon their oath aforesaid
present that; John Phillips, Larkin Eidson, George
Moore, John B. Riley, Swimpfield Anderson, Henry
S. War, Larkin M Kyle, Barnett Cantwell
Hiram Mills, David M Coy, Daniel S. McCulley
Hiram K Riley, William S Rose, Jacob Miller, Thomas
Moore, Calvin Jones, Abijah Anderson, George
Anderson, Hiram Tucker, Christian Tucker
Elbert Day, Westley Moore, Zachariah Biggs,
Jessee S. Leinsey, Gus Tegue, John Baker
Josiah Lawson, Woodson Wolf, Pleasent
Walker, John Brooks, James Jink David Cantwell,
Joseph Huffmaster, Swimpfield Eidson, George
Martin, Moses Anderson, Isaah Fain, John
Cantwell, James Forrester, Henry Rose, James
Long, William Moore, James Kyle, Christopher
Kyle, Stephen Thompson, Lipscome Parrott,
James Long, Calvin Baker and Abijah Manis
late of said County Hawkins laborers, not
having the fear of God before their Eyes but being
moved and seduced by the instigations of the
devil, did on the 7th day of December in the
year of our Lord one thousand Eight hundred
and Sixty one, in the County in and upon
one William Byrd in the peace of God, and
the State then and there being unlawfully
feloniously wilfully and of their Malice aforethought
make an assault, and that the said, John
Phillips, Larkin Eidson, George Moore,

John D. Riley, Swimpfield, Anderson, Henry S. Wax,
Larkin W. Kyle, Barnett Cantwell, Hiram Mills,
David McCoy, Daniel S. McCulley, Hiram K. Riley,
William S. Rose, Jacob Miller, Thomas Moore,
Calvin Jones, Abijah Anderson, George Anderson,
Hiram Tucker, Christian Tucker, Elbert Day,
Westley Moore, Zachariah Biggs, Jesse T. Levisay,
Gus Tegue, John Baker, Josiah Lawson,
Woodson Wolf, Pleasent Walker, John Brooks,
James Jink, David Cantwell, Joseph
Huffmaster, Swimpfield Eidson, George Martin,
Moses Anderson, Isaah Fain, John Cantwell,
James Forrester, Henry Rose, James Long, William
Moore, James Kyle, Cristopher Kyle, Stephen
Thompson, Lipscome, Parrott, James Long,
Calvin Baker, and Abijah Manis, with Guns
then and there loaded and charged with gun powder
and leaden balls, which said Guns, they the
said John Phillips, Larkin Eidson, George Moore,
John D. Riley, Swimpfield Anderson, Henry S. Wax,
Larkin W. Kyle, Barnett Cantwell, Hiram Mills,
David McCoy, Daniel S. McCulley, Hiram K. Riley,
William S. Rose, Jacob Miller, Thomas Moore,
Calvin Jones, Abijah Anderson, George Anderson,
Hiram Tucker, Christian Tuck[er]
Westley Moore, Zachariah Biggs, Jes[se]
Gus Tegue, John Baker, Josiah L[awson]
Wolf, Pleasent Walker, John Brow[ks]
David Cantwell, Joseph Huffmaster
Eidson, George Martin, Moses, An[derson]
Fain, John Cantwell, James Forrester,
James Long, William Moore, James
Kyle, Stephen Thompson, Lipscome
James Long, Calvin Baker, Abijah

in both their hands then and there had and held to
against and upon the said William Byrd, then and
there unlawfully feloniously, wilfully and of their malice
aforethought, did shoot and discharge and the said
John Phillips, Larkin Eidson, George Moore, John D. Riley,
Swimpfield Anderson, Henry S. Wax, Larkin W. Kyle,
Barnett Cantwell, Hiram Mills, David McCoy, Daniel
S. Coy, Daniel S. McCulley, Hiram K. Riley, William
S. Rose, Jacob Miller, Thomas Moore, Calvin Jones,
Abijah Anderson, George Anderson, Hiram Tucker,
Christian Tucker, Elbert Day, Westley Moore, Zachariah
Biggs, Jesse T. Levisay, Gus Tegue, John Baker, Josiah
Lawson, Woodson Wolf, Pleasent Walker, John
Brooks, James Jink, David Cantwell, Joseph Huffmaster,
Swimpfield Eidson, George Martin, Moses Anderson,
Isaah Fain, John Cantwell, James Forrester, Henry
Rose, James Long, William Moore, James Kyle,
Cristopher Kyle, Stephen Thompson, Lipscome,
Parrott, James Long, Calvin Baker, and Abijah Manis,
with the leaden balls aforesaid out of the guns aforesaid
then and by force of the gun powder shot and sent
forth, as aforesaid the said William Byrd, in and
upon the breast of him the said William Byrd
then and there feloniously wilfully and of their malice
aforethought did strike penetrate and wound, giving
[to] William Byrd one mortal wound, of
[the depth of ...] inches and of the breadth of
[... of] which said Mortal wound the said
[William Byrd ... died] on the day and year aforesaid
[in the County] aforesaid. And the
[Jurors ...] on their oath aforesaid, do say
[that the said] John Phillips, Larkin Eidson, George
[... Riley,] Swimpfield Anderson,
[Larkin] W. Kyle, Barnett Cantwell;

Joseph B. Heiskell, Eli Cox, James Gauntlem
Hiram Mills, David McCoy, Daniel S. McCulley, Hiram
K. Riley, William S. Rose, Jacob Miller, Thomas Moore,
Calvin Jones, Abijah Anderson, George Anderson, Hiram
Tucker, Christian Tucker, Elbert Day, Westley Moore,
Zachariah Biggs, Jesse T. Levisay, Gus Tegue, John
Baker, Josiah Lawson, Woodson Wolf, Pleasent
Walker, John Brooks, James Jink, David Cantwell,
Joseph Huffmaster, Swimpfield Eidson, George Martin,
Moses Anderson, Isaah Fain, John Cantwell, James
Forrester, Henry Rose, James Long, William Moore,
James Kyle, Cristopher Kyle, Stephen Thompson,
Lipscome, Parrott, James Long, Calvin Baker, and
Abijah Manis, the said William Byrd in manner
and form aforesaid feloniously wilfully premeditatedly
and of their malice aforethought did kill and
murder, to the evil example of all others in
like cases offending, and against the peace and
dignity of the State.

Men Sent to the Tuscaloosa, Alabama, Prison

Of the group of twenty-two men, including the ten men making court appearance with Ephraim Byrd, on January 24, 1862, only W.L. Richardson appears to have escaped the Tuscaloosa sentence, at least based on jailhouse notation.[226] A brief summary follows, combining jail, court, military and census information of the men sent to Tuscaloosa on Jan. 26, 1862:

- John Waddel, or Jno. Waddles on the jail list, is identified as John Waddle, age twenty, of War Creek, Holland District of Hancock County; arrested December 25, 1861, and member of Byrd's company.
- Edward S. McGinnis is identified as E.S. McGinnes, age twenty-five, of Lee Valley, District Two of Hawkins County; arrested December 10, 1861, and found to be with a union company, presumed to have been Byrd's. It must be noted that, in spite of the bleak circumstances caused by his Tuscaloosa sentencing, there is evidence Edward survived imprisonment and returned to Hawkins County sometime after July, 1862. But sadly, his father, Moses McGinnis records his young son's death in the family Bible on October 6, 1862.[227] What actually caused Edward's death is unknown, but it's conceivable his imprisonment may have played a significant role in young Edward's untimely demise.
- W.D. Cobb is believed to be Winstered Cobb, age forty-four, who lived in Lee Valley, District Two, Hawkins County. Cobb, a member of Byrd's company, was arrested on December 10, 1861.

- Eph. Bird, or Ephraim Byrd on the jail list, is identified in the census as Enoch Byrd, age twenty-seven, a farmer living in the War Creek area of Holland District, Hancock County. Arrested on December 12, 1861, he was the son of Captain William K. Byrd and found to be member of his father's company.
- N. Hurley, or just Harley on the list for Tuscaloosa, is believed to be Nehemiah Harley, age seventy-five, a farmer who lived in the Sneedville area, District Six of Hancock County. Arrested on December 14, 1861, Nehemiah was a member of Byrd's company and possibly a deserter from General Rosencrantz's group.
- Thomas Johnson is believed to be Thomas Johnson, as identified by the census, living in Lee Valley, Hawkins County, a few doors from Unionist Wintered (W.D.) Cobb. He could also be the same Thomas Johnson, as noted on the jail record and Tuscaloosa list. Johnson was taken into custody on December 25, 1861, being accused of membership in Byrd's company.
- Martin Murril, or Murrell on the jail list and Merrill on the Tuscaloosa list, is identified as Martin Murrel, age nineteen, a Lee Valley, Hawkins County resident and farm laborer who lived in the household of Rebecca Berton (Burton?). He was arrested on December 25, 1861, and was a member of Byrd's company.
- John D. Headrick, or "Hendrick" on the jail list. The jail record noted that this man was from Blount County, not Hancock or Hawkins, and was accused of being "in arms against C.S." Unfortunately, several John Headricks are noted as living in Blount County in the 1860 census, which prevents a positive identification. Also, there is a B.C. Headrick on the jail list—no county or age—who was "turned over to civil authorities." But closer to the Hawkins and Hancock area, other possibilities include John R. Headrick, age fifty-three, of St Clair area of District One, Hawkins County.[228] He might be the son of the same man, also named John, age sixteen, who later may have served with Company K, Fourth Tennessee Cavalry Regiment, USA.
- Jno (John) Harris may in fact be John Hanes, age thirty-five, of Sevier County, with a jail record noting him as a bridge burner and being sent to Tuscaloosa on January 26, 1861. But Hanes, as spelled, "is not on the separate list for Tuscaloosa for Jan 26." Another man, Jno. W. Harris, is on the jail record—having no age or county—who may be the same John Harris appearing in the court record and separate jail list going to Tuscaloosa. But strangely, this man, according to jail record, was "turned over to civil authorities." Adding further confusion, Jno. Harris could be

Jno. Hawes (Haines?), age thirty-five, who is on the jail list from Sevier County and was charged "with conveying letters to Lincoln's army," or John W. Harris, age twenty-four, son of widow Mary M. Harris, who lived in the St Clair area of District One, Hawkins County.[229] Of course, there was a man with the same name on the jail list but without age or county. Doubtless, this one remains very obscure.

- James T. Berry, or Ja. L. on the jail list and Ja. T. on the Tuscaloosa list, is identified as James Berry, age twenty-one, a resident of Lee Valley, Hawkins County. He was arrested and charged with shooting a member of Captain Phillips's E Company and being a suspected member of Byrd's company.

- W.L. Richardson. Unlike the others, Richardson may have ultimately avoided the Tuscaloosa sentence for one or more reasons. But it's noted that he is either William Richie, age eighteen, who lived in the Alanthus Hill area of the Four Mile District in Hancock County, or Willie Richards, age eighteen, of Mill Bend, District Four, Hawkins County, who lived with the Wm. Thomas family. The Knoxville jail record for "Richardson, Wm. L." gave his residence as Hancock County, age eighteen, having been arrested on December 9, 1861, for being a member of Byrd's company. After arrest, Richardson, according to yet another jail journal note, "enlisted with Lt. Hawkins SC [South Carolina], Jan. 18. 1862." But the same note added that Richardson had been sent to the hospital on January 19 and remains "here yet." A later, or second, jailhouse notation has Richardson still confined in the Knoxville jail as late as March 11, 1862. It also noted that "by order of Maj. Gen. Smith" (Edmund Kirby Smith), Richardson and nine other prisoners were to be "delivered to Lt Julius W. Rhett and mustered into [Confederate] service." Lieutenant Rhett appears to have been with the First Regiment South Carolina Artillery CSA unit, apparently serving in Tennessee at the time.

- W.V. Thompson is believed to be W.V. Thompson, age forty-six, of Hamilton County, a blacksmith by trade who lived near Limestone in District Five,[230] rather than W.P. Thompson, age forty-seven, of Meigs County or W.V. Thompson, as noted in two jail records. Plus, a search of the 1860 census for Meigs County failed to reveal a Thompson by the initials noted in the jail records. Also, jail data for W.P. Thompson listed him as a bridge burner and up in arms against the Confederate States. Interestingly, it appears that this same Thompson was sent to the hospital on January 7, 1862, only to later escape on January 26, the same day military authorities ushered his fellow prisoners off to Tuscaloosa, including a W.V. Thomson. But strangely, Thomson in the Tuscaloosa entry is also reported to have died at the hospital. In addition, it's known that a W.V. Thompson served in Captain David Fry's Company F, Second Tennessee Infantry, USA. So without additional information, Thompson's true identity will remain unclear.

- Tho (Thomas) Pickering is unidentified and didn't seem to reside in either Hawkins or Hancock Counties. No age or county is noted in his jail record, but he was sent with the others to Tuscaloosa on January 26, 1862.

- M. Cate is identified as Madison Cate, age thirty-six, a farmer and likely relative of J.H. Cate, who lived in the same district of Strawberry Plains, Sevier County.[231] Madison's jail record, like his suspected relative, listed him as a bridge burner and up in arms against the Confederate States. Madison Cate is also believed to be the same man described in William G. Brownlow's book, *Sketches of the Rise, Progress, and Decline of Secession; with a Narrative of Personal Adventures Among the Rebels*. In that work, Brownlow related a touching story of Madison's wife visiting him while he was lying near death in the Knoxville prison.[232]

- L. Cate is believed to be Enzord Cate, age thirty-seven, a farmer in the 1860 census, who lived in the Strawberry Plain area of the Twelfth District, Sevier County.[233] Enzord was accused of bridge burning and being up in arms against the Confederate States. His first name may have been John, who lived two doors from Madison Cate, a possible relative and fellow prisoner sent to Tuscaloosa. Another possibility is Lea Cate, age forty-two, of McMinn County, a well-to-do farmer who lived in the Calhoun area of District Eight.

- Ira Cate is believed to be J.H. Cate, age thirty-one, a farmer in the 1860 census, who lived in the Strawberry Plains area of District Twelve of Sevier County. On the jail list, J.H. is noted as J. Cate, but on the list going to Tuscaloosa, he appears to be identified as Ira Cate. Furthermore, J. Cate's jail record accused him of bridge burning, and Ira's census record had him as a close neighbor to Madison and Enzord Cate, with all three likely related and apparently accused of bridge burning.

- C.C. Howard is believed to be Columbus Howard, a laborer, age thirty, of Roane County, who lived in District Fourteen near Welcker Mills.[234] His jailhouse comments noted Howard as being up "in arms against C.S.," convicted by court-martial and of being an officer in Lincoln's army.

- P.B. Eldridge is identified in the 1860 census and jail record as J.B. Eldridge, age forty-seven. Only the separate list of men going to

Tuscaloosa on January 26 indicates his initials to be P.B.[235] J.B. resided in Meigs County, the Limestone area of District One and was a fairly well-to-do mechanic. J.B., supposedly for a time, according to court records, "was retained as a witness against other bridge burners."[236]

- Garrett Hall is believed to be Garrett Hall, age seventeen, of Morgan County, identified in the census as the young son of John Hall.[237] The Halls lived in District Four, near the Morgan County Courthouse. Authorities held Garrett at Knoxville as a prisoner of war only to send him later to Tuscaloosa with the others. Hall, like several jail prisoners and for reasons unclear, apparently had multiple jail records created, which obviously adds to the mystery surrounding each man's personal situation. For example, one of those records listed G. Hall, age forty-six, rather than seventeen, as noted in the census record. Again, this might be a simple jailhouse recording error or a reference to Hall being an older man, such as "Garrett Hall," age seventy-five, who also lived in Morgan County.

- Dan Smith is identified as Dan'l Smith, age sixty, a farmer who lived in the Timber Ridge area of District Twenty-five in Greene County.[238] Daniel, or Dan'l Smith as noted in the census, and Jacob Myers were convicted of involvement in the Lick Creek Bridge burning. Smith's jail record cited him a bridge burner.

- Joel Hogue, on the list going to Tuscaloosa, may also be Joel Hauge, age unknown, or Joel Hoge, age twenty-eight, both listed on the jail journal and from Rhea County. Of course, both appear to be duplicate entries or the same man, possibly another case of unexplained record duplication. Joel Hoge lived at Fillmore in the First Civil District. But maybe more noteworthy is the fact that Hauge's jail record noted him a "member of Cliff's [sic] company." A likely reference to Colonel William Clift, a Unionist leader and representative from Hamilton County to the Greeneville convention, who later served as colonel in the Fifth Tennessee Cavalry Regiment, USA. Clift, after receiving his commission from Union general George W. Morgan, was dispatched with his followers to Morgan and Scott Counties and told to "annoy the enemy's rear."[239] Of course, Hauge's jail entry noted him being sent to Tuscaloosa on January 26, 1862.

- Jacob Myers is identified in the census as Jacob Myars, age fifty, a well-to-do farmer, who lived in the Gustarus area of District Six of Greene County.[240] Myers, along with Dan or Daniel Smith of Greene County, were convicted of involvement in the Lick Creek Bridge burning. The jail journal had Jacob residing in Lee County, Virginia, at the time of his arrest.

Notes

INTRODUCTION

1. William K. Byrd may have spelled his surname with an "i" or "u" (e.g. Bird or Burd), rather a "y." Also, one child—maybe two—appears to have spent all or part of their lives spelling their surname "Bird." Four others seem to have preferred the "Byrd" spelling. For this work: William's surname is spelled with a "y," or "Byrd," while the surname spelling for his children are shown based on what seems to have been individual or personal preferences. Also, any general references to the Bird/Byrd family were done using the "Byrd" spelling. Various sources quoted in this work indicating a Bird, Burd or Byrd surname were quoted as written in the source material.

2. While North Carolina is indicated in one census (see 1920 Census note below), there is other evidence that points to Kentucky as being Byrd's birthplace. Recent DNA testing by one Byrd descendent has linked William K. Byrd to the Birds (spelled "Burd" by one source) in Barren County, Kentucky, about 1800–1810, who apparently migrated from South Carolina. 1920 U.S. census for King County, Seattle, Washington, for Levi B. Bird, Enumeration District 283, Sheet #17A, Ancestry.com (accessed August 28, 2004).

3. Pollyanna Creekmore, "Hawkins County Tennessee Tax List 1809–1812," chapter 8 in *Early East Tennessee Taxpayers, 1778–1839* (Easley, SC: Southern Historical Press, 1980), 161.

4. Maiden name taken from death certificate of Levi Benjamin Bird, youngest son of William K. Byrd. Washington State Board of Health, Bureau of Vital Statistics, November 3, 1924, Death Certificate record #2745, registration #2855.

5. Children's names and birth dates were taken from the following U.S. census records: 1850 for William Byrd, Hawkins County, Tennessee (District Three), 640; 1860 for Lias Bird, Hawkins County, Tennessee (District Two), 123; 1860 for Wm. E. Byrd, Hancock County, Tennessee (Holland District), 72. The exceptions are James Anderson Bird and Levi Benjamin Bird, whose pension papers were referenced.

1. PRELUDE TO TERROR

6. *Knoxville Register*, "Letter from Carter County," June 6, 1861.

7. Oliver Temple, *East Tennessee and the Civil War* (Reprint, Johnson City, TN: Overmountain Press, 1995), 347–48

8. Robert Tracy McKenzie, *Lincolnites and Rebels, A Divided Town in the American Civil War* (New York, Oxford University Press, 2006), 82.

9. David Madden, "Unionist Resistance to Confederate Occupation: The Bridge Burners of East Tennessee," *East Tennessee Historical Society's Publications* 52 and 53 (1980–1981), 23-24.

10. McKenzie, *Lincolnites and Rebels*, 89–90.

11. William G. Brownlow, *Sketches of the Rise, Progress, and Decline of Secession; with a Narrative of Personal Adventures Among the Rebels* (Philadelphia, PA: Applegate and Co., 1862), 134–40, 277–78, 299–301.

12. Madden, "Unionist Resistance," 22– 24.

13. McKenzie, *Lincolnites and Rebels*, 89–92

14. Temple, *East Tennessee*, 367

15. Thomas W. Humes, *The Loyal Mountaineers* (Reprint, Johnson City, TN: Overmountain Press, 1998), 133.

16. *Knoxville Register*, "Lincolnites in Carter," August 21, 1861.

17. Ibid., "The Capture of Dr. Thornburg," August 22, 1861.

18. Ibid, "Meeting in Hawkins County," May 2, 1861.

19. Ibid., "Arrival of the Hawkins Company," of May 16, 1861.

20. Army of Tennessee Records, AT-1-4-19, Record Group 4, Tennessee State Archives, Nashville, Tennessee, 157.

21. Ibid., AT-1-4-55, Record Group 4, 190.

22. *Knoxville Register*, "Hawkins on Hand," May 2, 1861.

23. Civil War Centennial Commission, *Tennesseans in the Civil War—Part 2* (Reprint, Knoxville: University of Tennessee Press, 2000), 349.

24. Eliza Rhea Anderson Fain Diary, vol. 1, book 7, July 24, 1861, H.B. Stamps Library, Rogersville, Tennessee, 87.

25. Noel C. Fisher, *War at Every Door: Partisan Politics & Guerrilla Violence in East Tennessee 1860–1869* (Chapel Hill: University of North Carolina Press, 1997), 42.

26. Alton L. Greene, "Hancock County Tennessee: "The County That Time Forgot," in *Hancock County Tennessee and Its People 1989* (Hancock County, Tennessee, Historical & Genealogical Society, 1989), 11–14.

27. Fisher, *War at Every Door*, 42.

28. *Knoxville Register*, "In the Confederate Court," September 12, 1861.

29. United States War Department, *The War of the Rebellion: A Compilation of the Official Records of the Union and Confederate Armies*, vol. 1, series 2 (Washington, D.C.: Government Printing Office, 1880–1899), 833.

30. W. Todd Groce, *Mountain Rebels, East Tennessee Confederates and the Civil War 1860–1870* (Knoxville: University of Tennessee Press, 2004), 110.

2. "INDISCRIMINATE ARRESTS"

31. McKenzie, *Lincolnites and Rebels*, 95–98.

32. William M. Robinson, *Justice in Grey: A History of the Judicial System of the Confederate States* (Cambridge, MA: Harvard University Press, 1941).

33. Court minutes, East Tennessee Confederate District Court at Knoxville, records for September 1861–May 1862, National Archives Southeast, Atlanta, Georgia, 2.

34. Ibid., 46.

35. Temple, *East Tennessee*, 405, 407, 409, 414–15.

36. McKenzie, *Lincolnites and Rebels*, 86, 114.

37. Temple, *East Tennessee*, 412–13.

38. Jacob A. Sperry, "Jos B. Heiskell," *Knoxville Register*, October 17, 1861.

39. McKenzie, *Lincolnites and Rebels*, 136.

40. Court minutes, 1–29.

41. U.S. Bureau of the Census, 1860, Hancock, Levicy, John McGee, 107.

42. Sheila Weems Johnston, comp., *The Blue and Gray, from Hawkins County Tennessee 1861–1865, The Federals* (Rogersville, TN: Hawkins County Genealogical and Historical Society, 1995), 1–67.

43. Civil War Pension Papers of James Anderson Bird, Master #739999, National Archives, Washington, D.C.

44. Court minutes, 9–10.

45. U.S. Bureau of the Census, 1860, Hancock County, Tennessee, Sixth District, Joel Jarvis, 89.

46. Sheila Weems Johnston, comp., *The Blue and Gray, from Hawkins County Tennessee, 1861–1865, The Confederates* (Rogersville, TN: Hawkins County Genealogical and Historical Society, 1995), 29.

47. Myers E. Brown II, *Images of America, Tennessee's Union Cavalrymen* (Charleston, SC: Arcadia Publishing, 2008), 80.

48. Jacob A. Sperry, *Knoxville Register*, "When Unionism Cost Tennessee," September 19, 1861.

49. Knoxville Register, "Arrival of Prisoners—An Escape," September 20, 1861. The article was reprinted from the *Union and American* in Nashville on September 17, 1861.

50. Court minutes, 4, 11–12, 15, 20–21.

51. William G. Brownlow, *Knoxville Whig*, "Indiscriminate Arrests," September 21, 1861.

52 *Knoxville Register*, "Arrests and Discharges," October 3, 1861. The information was reprinted from the *Athens Post*.

53. McKenzie, *Lincolnites and Rebels*, 93–95.

3. The Bridge Burnings

54. "Carter, whose ancestors figured prominently in the history of the region, was a pastor of a Rogersville church, but ill health forced him to retire from the ministry and he took over management of his family's farms. During the secession crisis, the forty-one year old minister spoke impressively against the evils of secession and supported the most extreme measures, including separate statehood for East Tennessee and armed resistance to the rebels." Madden, "Unionist Resistance," 25

55. Digby Gordon Seymour, *Divided Loyalties: Fort Sanders and the Civil War in East Tennessee* (Knoxville: University of Tennessee Press, 2002), 29.

56. Ibid., 36–37.

57. Temple, *East Tennessee*, 370–71.

58. Seymour, *Divided Loyalties*, 33–35.

59. Ibid., 35.

60. Richard Nelson Current, *Lincoln's Loyalists: Union Soldiers from the Confederacy* (Boston, MA: Northeastern University Press, 1992), 2–59.

61. Humes, *The Loyal Mountaineers*, 133.

62. Seymour, *Divided Loyalties*, 29.

63. Temple, *East Tennessee*, 400–03.

64. Ibid., 390–92.

65. Donahue Bible, *Broken Vessels, The Story of the "Pottertown" Bridge Burners, November–December, 1861*, 2nd edition (Mohawk, TN: Dodson Creek Publishers., 1997).

66. Donahue Bible, "The Hangings of the Greene County Bridge Burners," *Tennessee Ancestors, A Tri-Annual Publication of the East Tennessee Historical Society* (August 2005), 130 – 139.

67. Temple, *East Tennessee*, 390.

68. Humes, *The Loyal Mountaineers*, Appendix X.

4. They "Drew the Vengeance of the Rebels"

69. Fain Diary, vol. 1, book 9, November 24, 1861, 99.

70. Civil War Centennial Commission, *Tennesseans in the Civil War—Part 1* (Reprint, Knoxville: University of Tennessee, 2000), 469.

71. Civil War Pension Papers of Levi Benjamin Bird, Master #740054, National Archives, Washington, D.C.

72. Bruce E. Johnson, "8th Tennessee Cavalry Regiment (US)," *Our Mountain Heritage* 14, no. 1 (Winter 2002), 5.

73. Jack H. Goins, *Melungeons, Footprints from the Past* (Rogersville, TN: self-published, 2009), 162–63. This contains comments relating to Larkin Stapleton's Civil War pension papers.

74. Wm. Miller, "Affidavit of Wm. Miller of the US Pension Office, May 11, 1881," Civil War Pension Papers of James Anderson Bird, Master #739999, National Archives, Washington, D.C., 2.

75. The "Lincolnist" or "Lincolnites" label was used sometimes by Confederate authorities and supporters in a hateful or derogatory sense to refer to anyone who supported the Union and/or President Lincoln.

76. *William D. Trent v. Robert Kyle & J.W. Phillips*, August 7, 1866, Hancock County Chancery Court, microfilm, H.B Stamps Library, Rogersville, Tennessee, 2,126–30.

77. Crawford W. Hall, *Threescore Years and Ten* (Cincinnati, OH: Elm Street Printing Co., 1884), 143.

78. Dickson Family Letters, Private Collection of George E. Webb Jr., Hawkins County; *Distant Crossroads* 21, no. 4 (2004), 109–11.

79. Johnston, *The Blue and Gray, The Confederates*, 189–93.

80. Hall, *Threescore Years and Ten*, 143.

81. War Record of Wylie Miller Young, Civil War Collection MF-AC No. 1489, Tennessee State Archives, Nashville, Tennessee.

82. Civil War Centennial Commission, *Tennesseans in the Civil War—Part 1*, 268

83. Grand Jury Indictment for the Murder of William K. Byrd, October Term 1865, Hawkins County Circuit Court Records, H.B Stamps Library, Rogersville, Tennessee.

5. Confrontation: The Byrd Raid

84. John N. Fain, ed., *Hiram Fain of Rogersville, His Diary—Long Version, 1850–1870*, transcript, H.B Stamps Library, Rogersville, Tenn., 34.

85. Fain Diary, vol. 1, book 9, December 5, 1861, 100.

86. Ibid., December 6, 1861, 100.

87. U.S. Bureau of the Census, 1860, Hawkins, Tennessee; Second District, James A. William and Lias Bird, 123.

88. Ibid., Hancock, Tennessee, Holland District, Jackson and Enoch Byrd, 77.

89. Fain Diary, vol. 1, book 9, Dec. 26, 1861, 100–101.

90. Hall, *Threescore Years and Ten*, 143.

91. Grand Jury Indictment for the murder of William K. Byrd.

92. Hall, *Threescore Years and Ten*, 143.

93. *William D. Trent v. Robert Kyle & J.W. Phillips*, 2,152.

94. Dickson Family Letters, 109.

6. The Arrests Begin

95. Dorothy E. Kelly, transcriber, "Sent to Tuscaloosa, East Tennessee Civilians in the Knoxville Jail," *Tennessee Ancestors, A Tri-Annual Publication of the East Tennessee Historical Society*

(December 2007), 127–44. According to Ms. Kelly, jail information was transcribed from Confederate War Records, National Archives, Record 109, chapter 9, vol. 219½.

96. U.S. Bureau of the Census, 1860, Hancock, Tennessee, Holland District, James and Joseph Green, 77.

97. Ibid., Hawkins, Tennessee, Lee Valley (District Three), L.W. Itson, 93.

98. William R. Snell, ed., *Myra Inman, A Diary of the Civil War in East Tennessee* (Macon, GA: Mercer University Press, 2000), 137, 139.

99. U.S. Bureau of the Census, 1860, Hancock, Tennessee, Four Mile District, William Richie, 174.

100. Ibid., Hawkins, Tennessee, District Four, Willie Richards, 184.

101. Ibid., District Two, Cobb, J.D (Jesse) and James Berry and McGinnis, 121, 124, 126.

102. Ibid., Hancock, Sumpter and Walker Districts, John Wolf, John Wolf, 57, 153.

103. Ibid., District Six, Abram Hopkins, Ephraim and Jackson Byrd and Nehemiah and Moses Hurley, 14, 17, 23, 77.

104. Ibid., Hawkins, District Two, Martin Murrel, 121.

105. Temple, *East Tennessee*, 399.

106. U.S. Bureau of the Census, 1860, Hancock, District Six, George M. Daughtry, 11.

107. Ibid., Holland, John Waddle, Stephen Frost and William Buttery, 74, 76, 81.

108. Ibid., Walker, William B. Jones, 57.

109. Ibid., Davis, Alfred Brooks, 89, 91.

110. Ibid., Holland, George W. Trent, 82.

111. Ibid., Hawkins, District Two, John Wright, 110.

112. Ibid., District Thirteen, John Wright, 141.

113. Ibid., District Fourteen, Marion, Horry and Emberson Walker, 64

7. CASTLE FOX PRISON, THEN THE TRIALS

114. McKenzie, *Lincolnites and Rebels*, 103–04.

115. William G. Brownlow, *Sketches of the Rise, Progress, and Decline of Secession, with a Narrative of Personal Adventures Among the Rebels* (Philadelphia, PA: Applegate and Co, 1862), 303–08.

116. Brownlow, *Sketches of the Rise*, 312–19.

117. Court minutes, 32–44.

118. Ibid., 45–51.

119. Ibid., 73–75.

120. Ibid., 76–77.

121. Court minutes, 76.

122. U.S. Bureau of the Census, 1860, Hancock, Davis, John Willbourn, 89.

123. Kelly, transcriber, "Sent to Tuscaloosa," 133.

124. Ibid., 143–44.

125. Ibid., 133, 143–44, 135–36.

126. Ibid., 135–36.

127. U.S. Bureau of the Census, 1860, Hawkins, District Two, James Buttery, 123.

128. Ibid., Hancock, John G. Levicy and John Levicy, 106–07.

129. Kelly, transcriber, "Sent to Tuscaloosa," 136, 143–44.

130. U.S. Bureau of the Census, 1860, Sevier, District Twelve, Jas Hickman, 57.

131. Ibid., District Eight, Harvey Langston, 47.

132. Ibid., Hawkins, District Twelve, Richard Robinson, 164.

133. Ibid., Hancock, John McGee Levicy, 107.

134. Johnston, *The Blue and Gray, The Confederates*, 33–34.

135. U.S. Bureau of the Census, 1860, Hancock, Wm Goens Murrel, 66.

136. Kelly, transcriber, "Sent to Tuscaloosa," 143–44.

137. Dr. Robert Mellown, "Tuscaloosa During the Civil War," Historic Tuscaloosa, www.historictuscaloosa.org/civilwar.html.

8. PROFILE OF A RAIDING PARTY

138. John Trotwood Moore and Austin P. Foster, *Tennessee, The Volunteer State, 1769–1923*, vol. 3 (Chicago, IL: S.J. Clarke Publishing Co, 1923), 191.

139. James B. Jones Jr., ed., Tennessee Civil War Sourcebook, http://tennessee.civilwarsourcebook.com. Search argument, "Heiskell."

140. Temple, *East Tennessee*, 412–13.

141. To answer possible questions regarding authorship of the August 8, 1866 article attributed to William G. Brownlow, a second or previous article exists, also published in the *Whig*, dated August 31, 1864. It was written only days after Heiskell's capture, which make the same scathing, almost identical, accusations regarding Heiskell as the later August 8, 1866 article. While authorship goes unrecorded on both *Whig* articles, both bear the unmistakable flair and stamp of a William G. Brownlow article, providing basis for attributing both articles to Brownlow.

142. William G. Brownlow, "Capture of Joseph B. Heiskell," *Knoxville Whig*, August 8, 1866.

143. Hall, *Threescore Years and Ten*, 143.

144. *William D. Trent v. Robert Kyle & J. W. Phillips*, 2,030.

145. Ibid., 2,126–30.

146. William G. Brownlow, "Capt. Joseph Hoffmaster (*sic*)," *Knoxville Whig*, December 14, 1864.

147. *William D. Trent v. Robert Kyle & J. W. Phillips*, 2,226–27.

148. U.S. Bureau of the Census, 1860, Hancock, Sixth District, Nelson Seal, 17.

149. *William D. Trent v. Robert Kyle & J. W. Phillips*, 2,117–81.

150. Johnston, *The Blue and Gray, The Confederates*, 81–91.

151. *William D. Trent v. Robert Kyle & J. W. Phillips*, 2,032–33.

152. Phillip Shaw Paludan, *Victims: A True Story of the Civil War* (Knoxville: University of Tennessee Press, 1981), 66–68.

153. Fain Diary, vol. 1, book 9, March 27, 1862, 106.

154. John N. Fain, ed., *Sanctified Trial, The Diary of Eliza Rhea Anderson Fain, a Confederate Women in East Tennessee* (Knoxville: University of Tennessee Press, 2004), 364–65.

9. MEETING AT NEW MARKET, TENNESSEE

155. Confederate Papers Relating to Citizens or Business Firms, 1861–1865, NARA publication M346, Catalog Id 213374, Record Group 109, document #248, National Archives, Washington, D.C.

156. Kenneth C. Martis, *The Historical Atlas of the Congress of the Confederate States of America 1861–1865* (New York: Simon & Schuster, 1994), 32.

157. United States War Department, *The War of the Rebellion*, vol. 39, part 1, reports, 484–92.

158. Samuel W. Scott and Samuel P. Angel, *History of the Thirteenth Regiment, Tennessee Volunteer Cavalry, U.S.A.* (Philadelphia, 1903; reprinted, Johnson City, TN: Overmountain Press, 1987), 158–59.

159. Sheila Weems Johnston, comp., *The Blue and Gray, from Hawkins County, Tennessee, The Battles* (Rogersville, TN: Hawkins County Genealogical and Historical Society, 1995), 35–37. The original information was published in the *Confederate Magazine*, 1893–1932.

160. Steve Humphrey, *"That D——d Brownlow," Being a Sancy & Malicious Description of Fighting Parson William Gannaway Brownlow*, Boone, NC: Appalachian Consortium Press, 1978, 345.

161. United States War Department, *The War of the Rebellion*, 299–303.

162. Ibid., series 1, vol. 39, part 2, Correspondence, Etc., 311.

163. Brownlow, "Capture of A. G. Watkins," *Knoxville Whig*, August 24, 1864.

164. Union Provost Marshals File of Papers Relating to Individual Citizens, No:MF-AC.1047, Microfilm copy 345, roll 123, Haz-Hei group, Tennessee State Archives, Nashville, Tennessee.

165. United States War Department, *The War of the Rebellion*, series 2, Prisoners of War, vol. 7, 1,111–15.

166. Ibid., 1,183–84.

167. Ibid., 1,229.

168. Groce, *Mountain Rebels*, 125.

169. Fisher, *War at Every Door*, 150–53.

170. United States War Department, *The War of the Rebellion*, series 2, Prisoners of War, vol. 8, 272–74.

171. Johnston, *The Blue and Gray, The Battles*, 56–58.

172. United States War Department, *The War of the Rebellion*, series 2, Prisoners of War, vol. 8, 380–81.

173. Selected Records of the War Department Relating to Confederate POW's 1861–1865, Release of Prisoners, microfilm roll #8, M598, from the East Tennessee Historical Center, Knoxville, Tennessee, 66.

10. Indictments for Murder and Treason

174. Fain, *Sanctified Trial*, lxiii.

175. Grand Jury Indictment for the Murder of William K. Byrd, October Term 1865.

176. Fain Diary, vol. 1, book 9, March 27, 1862, 106.

177. Civil War Centennial Commission, *Tennesseans in the Civil War—Part 2*, 216–21.

178. Copies of Legal Summons and Wits Involving Joseph B. Heiskell, October Term 1865–January Term 1867, Hawkins County Circuit Court, Hawkins County Archives Building, Rogersville, Tennessee.

179. Hawkins County Genealogical and Historical Society, *Hawkins County Tennessee Marriages 1866–1899* (Maryville, TN: Stinnett Printing, 1997), 32.

180. *Knoxville Register*, "The Unionist in Eastern Tennessee," November 19, 1861.

181. Fain, *Sanctified Trial*, lxv-lxvi.

182. John N. Fain, "Nicholas Fain: An Irish Emigrant and Nicholas Fain of Rogersville," *Distant Crossroads* 13, no. 2 (1996), 54–57.

183. *Vaughan, John v. Philips, John*, July Term 1865, microfilm roll #2337 Vol. Si-Yo 1861–1870, Hawkins County Circuit Court, H.B Stamps Library, Rogersville, Tennessee.

184. Grand Jury Indictment of John Philips for treason, October Term 1865, microfilm roll #2337 Vol. Si-Yo 1861–1870, Hawkins County Circuit Court, H.B Stamps Library, Rogersville, Tennessee.

11. Search for Justice Continues

185. *Andrew J. Byrd Adm. of Wm. Byrd decd. v. George Moore, Swimpfield Anderson & others*, February 1, 1866, Hawkins County Circuit Court, 617.

186. Ibid., June 6, 1866, 91.

187. Ibid., October 1, 1867, 148–49.

188. Ibid., October 8, 1868, 210–11.

189. Ibid., January 28, 1869, 249.

190. Ibid., September 1869, 617.

191. Ibid., September 27, 1869, 231.

192. Ibid., September 26, 1871.

193. Ibid., September 28, 1876.

194. Ibid., February 4, 1878.

12. HANCOCK-HAWKINS COUNTIES— :A BRIDGE BURNING CONNECTION?

195. Bible, "The Hangings," 130.

13. WAS IT CONSPIRACY AND MURDER OR A MILITARY ENGAGEMENT?

196. Paludan, *Victims: A True Story*, 84–98.

197. Ibid., 67–68.

198. Fain, *Sanctified Trial*, lxiii.

199. Thomas Benjamin Alexander, *Thomas A.R. Nelson of East Tennessee* (Nashville: Tennessee Historical Commission, 1956).

200. Thomas Benjamin Alexander, "Strange Bedfellows: The Interlocking Careers of T.A.R. Nelson, Andrew Johnson, and W.G. (Parson) Brownlow." *East Tennessee Historical Society's Publications* 51 (1979): 54–77.

201. Henry R. Price, *Hawkins County Tennessee: A Pictorial History* (Virginia Beach, VA, Donning Company Publishers, 1996), 107–13.

202. *Knoxville Register*, "The Unionist in Eastern Tennessee," November 19, 1861.

203. Ibid., "Hon. Jos. B. Heiskell," December 26, 1861, 2.

204. Compiled Service Records of Confederate General and Staff Officers and Non-Regimental Enlisted Men, NARA publication M331, Catalog Id 586957, Record Group 109, dated November 6, 1863, National Archives, Washington, D.C.

205. Henry R. Price, *Old Rogersville: An Illustrated History of Rogersville, Tennessee* (Rogersville, TN: self-published, 2002), 157–58.

14. CLOSING REFLECTIONS

206. "Joseph Brown Heiskell–Pardon Petition," Center for Legislative Archives, Record Group 233, U.S. House of Representatives, Select Committee on Reconstruction, Applications for the Removal of Legal and Political Disabilities of Tennessee, HR 40A-H21.19, Application No. 14041, National Archives, Washington, D.C.

207. John Trotwood Moore and Austin P. Foster, *Tennessee: The Volunteer State, 1769-1923*, vol. 3, records 682–701, Ancestry.com.

208. A.A. Kyle Ledger Book 1860–1884, Hawkins County, Tennessee, Genealogical and Historical Society, as published in *Distant Crossroads* 18, no. 1 (2001), 24.

209. Moore and Foster, *Tennessee, The Volunteer State*, records 682–701.

210. U.S. Bureau of the Census, 1880, Washington County, Arkansas, Mountain Township, Enumeration district 210, family of John W. and Jane Phillips, 613.

211. Ibid., 1900, Washington County, Arkansas, Valley Township, Enumeration district 117, family of John R. and Carrie Phillips, 342

212. Barbara P Easley, comp., *Obituaries of Washington County Arkansas, Volume 3, 1903–1908* (Bowie MD: Heritage Books, Inc., 1996), 300–01.

213. Ike (Isaac) Fain affidavit, dated Oct. 7, 1867, in the case of *State of Tenn. v. Eidson, Larkin; Martin, George; Phillips, John et al.*, the 1865 murder (Civil War) Byrd, William, stored in folder 2 of 2, Hawkins County Circuit Court, Hawkins County Archives Building, Rogersville, Tennessee.

214. Fain, *Sanctified Trial*, 361.

215. Minutes of the Richardson Creek Baptist Church, Hawkins County, 1886–1887, H.B. Stamps Library, Rogersville, Tennessee.

216. Judgments Rendered, *State v. William E. Byrd, Robbery*, February 2, 1866, Hawkins County Circuit Court, 278, entry 502.

217. Civil War Pension Papers of Levi Benjamin Bird, Master #740054, National Archives, Washington, D.C.

218. Affidavits of Joseph R. Buttery and James C. Burton, December 6, 1878, Civil War Pension Papers of James Anderson Bird, Master #739999, National Archives, Washington, D.C., 71–77.

219. During the Civil War, a sutler, sometimes spelled "sutter," followed an army or maintained a store on an army post to sell provisions to soldiers.

220. Civil War Pension Papers of James Anderson Bird.

221. *Kyle's Ford Quadrangle, Tenn.-Va.* map, dated 1947 (revised in 1969), U.S. Department of Interior Geological Survey.

222. Groce, *Mountain Rebels*, 133.

223. Ibid., 138–41.

224. Ibid., 140–41.

225. Abraham Fulkerson, "Sixty-third Tennessee Infantry," in *The Military Annals of Tennessee, Confederate: First Series: Embracing a View of Military Operations*, edited by John Berrien Lindsley (Nashville, TN: J.M. Lindsley, 1886), 584–95.

APPENDIX B

226. Kelly, "Sent to Tuscaloosa," 136.

227. Hallie Price Garner, *The Descendants of Peter Paul Jones of Hawkins County, Tennessee* (Dallas, TX: self-published, 2009), 17–18, 30.

228. U.S. Bureau of the Census, 1860, Hawkins, District One, John R. Headrick, 73.

229. Ibid., John R. Harris, 78.

230. Ibid., Hamilton, District Nine, W.V. Thompson, 35.

231. Ibid., Sevier, District Twelve, Madison Cate, 56.

232. Brownlow, *Sketches of the Rise*, 326–29.

233. U.S. Bureau of the Census, 1860, Sevier, District Twelve, Emzord and J.H. Cate, 56–57.

234. Ibid., Roane, District Fourteen, Columbus Howard, 277.

235. Ibid., Meigs, District One, J.B. Eldridge, 11.

236. Kelly, "Sent to Tuscaloosa," 129.

237. U.S. Bureau of the Census, 1860, Morgan, District Four, Garrett Hall, 38.

238. Ibid., Greene, District Twenty-five, Dan't Smith, 108.

239. Fisher, *War at Every Door*, 38, 42, 54, 64, 73.

240. U.S. Bureau of the Census, 1860, Greene, District Six, Jacob Myars, 188.

Index

About the Author

Marvin J. Byrd is a graduate of Oral Roberts University, 1974, with a bachelor's of science in business administration. Born in Oklahoma City and raised in Tulsa, Marvin has always had a deep love and appreciation for American history, especially the Civil War era. Until a few years ago, he never dreamed of writing a book, much less publishing one on the Civil War. But beginning in the 1980s, Marvin began researching his family history, starting with only the names of his grandparents written on a piece of paper found among his deceased father's personal papers. Using this information, he located his grandfather's obituary in the archives of the local paper where he learned of his granddad's birth in 1860 in Lee Valley, Tennessee.

From there, it wasn't until 2002, while conversing with a newly discovered cousin living in Harrison, Arkansas, that he learned of his great-great-grandfather's death at the hands of Confederate sympathizers. With this knowledge sparking his interest, Marvin set out on what became an eight-year journey to learn all he could about the events and circumstances surrounding his great-great-grandfather's death. This effort culminated in *A Unionist in East Tennessee: Captain William K. Byrd and the Mysterious Raid of 1861*.

Prior to *A Unionist in East Tennessee*, Marvin published two previous articles with the Hawkins County Genealogical and Historical Society, located in Rogersville, Tennessee—one on Byrd family history, "William Elliott and Susannah (Templeton) Byrd and Descendants," and the other, "Levi Benjamin Bird," which details the life and civil war service of Captain Byrd's youngest son.

Marvin spent forty-three years working in information technology in the oil industry in Tulsa and Houston, Texas. He retired from the Hess Corporation in 2008. Marvin and his wife, Mary, live in the Tulsa area and have three children and eight grandchildren.